SEASONAL PRAYERS

MEDITATIONS ON THE EPISTLES

of

The Act of Consecration of Man

Alan Stott

CLAIRVIEW

Clairview Books Ltd.,
Russet, Sandy Lane,
West Hoathly,
W. Sussex RH19 4QQ

www.clairviewbooks.com

Published by Clairview Books 2025

Previously published in an earlier version by Anastasi Ltd. 2013

A CIP catalogue record for this book is available from the British Library

ISBN 978 1 912992 77 5

Cover by Morgan Creative
Typeset by Symbiosys Technologies, Visakhapatnam, India
Printed and bound by 4Edge Ltd, Essex

Contents

Thomas Aquinas and Albertus Magnus
19th century painting in the Dominican Priory, Albertinium, Fribourg,
Switzerland

Preface

*'I will pray with the spirit, and I will pray with the understanding also:
I will sing with the spirit, and I will sing with the understanding also.'*
(1 Cor. 14:15)

'Ears hast Thou dug (bored) for me.' (Ps. 40:6 Heb.)

John Mason Neale

IT is often said that those who do not find the books for which they are searching should try writing their own. Amateur ('lay') exponents of Scripture—the Church's possession—have been deplored since Jerome's day in the fifth century. Well, in the periods between musical activity, offering and occasionally being asked to play for The Act of Consecration of Man—the Eucharist of the 'Movement for Religious Renewal', The Christian Community—I have been exploring the theological, spiritual and devotional literature in English of the Michael Age and of the period immediately prior to 1879—forerunners include the indefatigable John Mason Neale (1818-1866, photo: above) of East Grinstead, historian, hymnologist, commentator and born storyteller, who almost single-handedly founded liturgiology. An undreamt richness met me, by no means lacking in what Paul terms 'understanding'. My experience of several men of prayer brought into fresh clarity the question of contemporary religious renewal. This involves not only the question of recognizing in myself (naiveté notwithstanding) Pharisaical and Sadducean extremes—tendencies well-known to students of anthroposophy under their cosmic, personal names.

Over the years, occasional articles of mine have appeared in *Die Christengemeinschaft*, *The Threshing Floor* and *Perspectives*. Encouraged by my friends, the following elementary

1

meditations (using the word in its generally accepted meaning as itself a form of prayer)—originally intended for the journal *Perspectives* and encouraged by the editor Tom Ravetz—were first distributed to the priests of The Christian Community, those to whom responsibility rests for the spoken liturgy. Since then, I have been eager to learn of research by speech-artists, musicians and priests—who all face the task of renewal. I was brought up to learn from others and to share. Research is more than a buzz-word. Although Academia is supposed to be free of the claims of churchmanship, or the denominations, one can notice fashions, human failings, assumptions and certain patronizing attitudes. However, 'the Sun is … the source of all intellectual life', claims our main Church Father, Rudolf Steiner (Torquay, 21 Aug. 1924, GA 240). Spiritual activity is what unites us all, despite any exclusive claims, and indeed including the counterclaims of the anti-intellectuals.

Clearly, in the chosen text conceived as a series, some things will appear more than once. Since these attempts were penned—one chapter a day and a couple of weeks spent revising the draft—I have met only serious seekers who were interested in the subject. In what follows, numerical observations always refer to the original German text, published last century (GA 345, Dornach 1994). The texts are also published in Günther Dellbrügger, *Im Herzeland* (Urachhaus, Stuttgart 2014/16; Eng. tr. forthcoming). Granted that liturgies are to be *heard*, with bona fide research it is well known there are *no* visa restrictions, sell-by date, membership clauses or small print. George Matheson, the 'blind seer of Scotland' whose unique contributions began to appear and cause a stir from 1878, claims, 'Devotion is not the absence of thought, and thought is not necessarily the absence of devotion.' These words struck a chord; one attempt written to meet the needs of another century is in your hands.

I warmly thank my friends for help in producing this booklet on the Epistles—'the wives of the Apostles', as Dr Rudolf Köhler, a founder priest of The Christian Community, once affirmed with a twinkle of his eye. This booklet originally appeared in a limited edition during the celebrations for the new millennium.

Hans-Werner Schroeder, a tutor at the Priests Seminary, Stuttgart, who went on to write his own suggestive introduction *Die Episteln der Menschenweihehandlung* (Urachhaus, Stuttgart 2009), suggested (2003) to the Editors of *Die Christengemeinschaft* monthly journal that in his opinion my little book is '*a valuable stimulus. It contains many thoughts which are wide-ranging and useful ...*'; Herr Schroeder's own contribution of 2009 is not referred to in my text of 1999. Taco Bay (photo: below), *Erzoberlenker* ('Head Steersman' or 'Head Co-ordinator') of The Christian Community with worldwide responsibility, wrote in English to the present writer (21 Feb. 2001):

Taco Bay

'*... a very sincere thank-you for the little booklet that you have written and published on the Epistles of The Act of Consecration of Man. You have trodden ground that hitherto no one else has dared to do regarding this most remarkable sequence of prayers. To me they are a revelation of Christ as He would reveal Himself in our time. Your approach as a musician and relating them to the Psalter is novel and as impressive as it would be from any other angle too. Dr Frieling would have enjoyed your study of numbers which were a part of his approach to sacred texts. Additionally, you show great interest in placing it in relation to other biblical writings and in quoting many learned theologians. All in all, it makes quite a fascinating little work full of weighty content....* [At a forthcoming meeting, I hope to meet in order] *to express my regard and joy of what you so courageously have put on paper ...*'

The late Rev. George Klockner kindly allowed me to use one of his diagrams of the yearly cycle. Maria Ver Eecke, Neil Franklin, Ph.D. and Christopher & Raphaela Cooper made many helpful comments. I have endeavoured to be accurate; responsibility and all remaining shortcomings are mine. The German texts—to repeat, the facsimile in GA 345 was essential for all contemplations and calculations in writing these studies—have been available for thirty years. The facts remain: Scripture and Liturgy are the property of the Church, which some say began life with the calling of Abram.

The cover picture of an angelic army (precisely 17 angels—the number of God's covenanted people) is from a panel by Guariento Rodolfo (c. 1370) in the City Museum of Padua (Photo: Scala, Florence. Available as postcard No. 1319 and as a print from Raffael-Verlag, Stockhornstr. 5, CH-3863 Ittigen).

Alan Stott, Michaelmas 1999,
updated Michaelmas 2013 & 2024

AV = the Jacobean translation, or the Authorized
   [= to be read in churches] / King James Version
GNB = Good News Bible (to be avoided—see Prickett 1986)
NJB = New Jerusalem Bible
KV = Ronald Knox Version
LXX = Greek Septuagint of the OT
NIV = New International Version
PBV = Prayer Book Version
REB = Revised English Bible
RSV = Revised Standard Version
RV = Revised Version (1881; the most accurate word-for-word
   translation)
WB = William Barclay's trans. of the New Testament (1968/69)

Charles C. Torrey *The Four Gospels* (1933; in English, corrected by reconstructing the Aramaic original)

Das Neue Testament, tr. Heinrich Ogilvie (1996), *The Translator's NT* (1973); The NT tr. by Richmond Lattimore (1969); *The Original NT*, tr. Hugh J. Schonfield (rev. ed. 1985; Element, Shaftesbury 1988); and *The Message* (NT paraphrase) by Eugene H. Peterson (Colorado Springs: Navpress 2003), are all worth knowing.

Seasonal Prayers: The Epistles of The Act of Consecration of Man

'Pray without ceasing.' (1 Thess. 5:17).

THE Christian Church over the centuries has enriched its liturgy with seasonal additions. Many of the psalms, antiphons, Epistles (New Testament readings), sentences, hymns and collects—a feature of the Western Church—are instructive, beautiful and appropriate. Thomas Aquinas, for example, composed the liturgy for *Corpus Christi* and several admired liturgical hymns. Liturgical experiment, revision and renewal continue in our own day.[1] In The Act of Consecration of Man, the Eurcharist of The Christian Community (founded in 1922) we are privileged to hear seasonal, liturgical Epistles (twelve sets in all, counting Easter Week and three for Christmas) that raise liturgical enrichment to an entirely new level. Their position in the unfolding sequence is significant. We approach and leave the ever repeated yet constantly developing Act at the altar, as it were, through the changing doorway of the present seasonal moment. In addition, the Inserted Prayer which speaks of intimate and even dramatic inner events, prepares for the movement of the Offertory—except for the Epistles for Christmas and St John's Tide, which come after the Offertory.

The human being, we learn in the *Tanakh*, our 'Old Testament', looks at the outward appearance, but Yahweh ('He who causes to be'), the Saviour God of the Old Testament, looks into the heart (1 Sam. 16:7). Yahweh puts His Law, His Word, not on tablets of stone but in the minds of His people, 'on their hearts' (Heb. 8:10 and Jer. 31:33), which He fashions in the first place (Ps. 33:15). In the Bible, the heart for the most part is synonymous for the centre of the personality, or the personality as a whole. It is 'the sharp dividing line between our mortal and our immortal part' (John Oman). It is 'the Holy Palace' or 'the Inward Palace' of Jewish tradition. The heart is a profound organ of perception in the body. We identify the heart as the central organ of the feelings, of our humanity. The seasonal Epistles speak of the deep experience of the heart. We hear of the life of the Trinity and the beings of the spiritual world who are directly concerned with humanity. By appealing to our awareness, the Epistles verbalize our present experience and lead it further. They offer a schooling in living 'the eternal present'. We are helped to 'lift up' our hearts, as the ancient Latin Preface puts it, responding (literally) 'we have them with the Lord'. The substance of this benediction is found in Ruth 2:4, Ps. 129:8 and 2 Thess. 3:16. We experience sonship. 'God sent the Spirit of his Son in our hearts' (Gal. 4:6); we are children of God by adoption (Rom. 8:14-17). In his very first article, George Matheson (1842-1906), the blind seer of Scotland, wrote: 'The Master conceived the grand design of establishing a kingdom that could never be moved … whose foundation was the nature of humanity itself—the capacity for love. He proposed to conquer the heart of the world, and to conquer it by the exhibition of his own heart.' The life of the intimate Christian Mysteries contained in the new liturgical Epistles, like the human heart itself, is inexhaustible.

Over one hundred years ago, Father Benson (1824-1915), founder of the Cowley Fathers, expressed in few words much that is more fully unfolded in the Epistles:

> It is little that we should have given ourselves to Him—the marvel is that our gift of ourselves is but an echo of His loving call; and while we give ourselves to Him with hearts so dull and eyes so blind, He gives Himself to us that He may quicken our hearts, until our eyes are opened to behold what at present we can only know by faith [Father R.M. Benson, letter to Brother Herbert, August, 1898].

> *Give me, O Lord, a steadfast heart*
> *which no unworthy affection may drag downwards;*
> *Give me an unconquered heart,*
> *which no tribulation can wear out;*
> *Give me an upright heart,*
> *which no unworthy purpose may tempt aside;*

Bestow upon me also, O Lord, my God,
understanding to know Thee
diligence to seek Thee
wisdom to find Thee
and a faithfulness that may finally embrace Thee.
    [prayer of Thomas Aquinas]

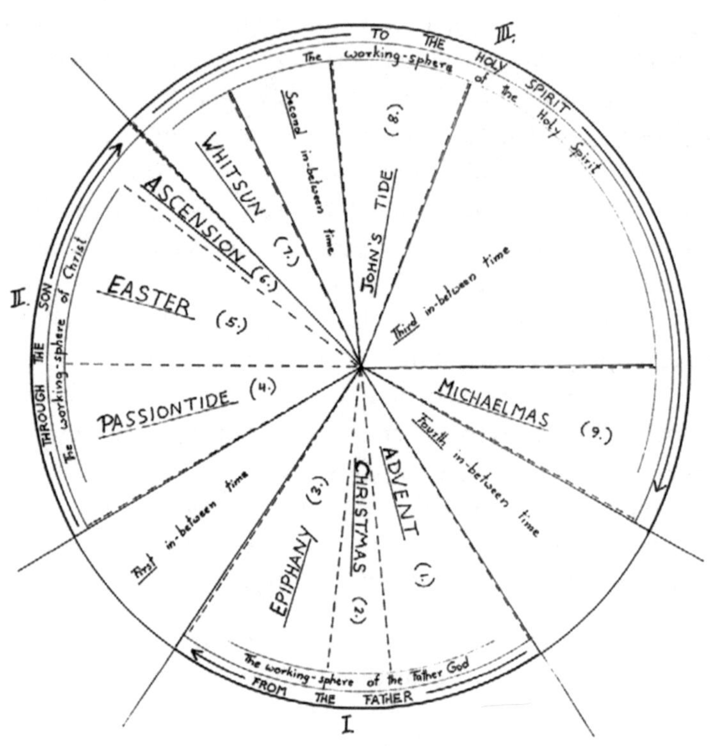

Cycle of Festivals

ADVENT

Our souls fall deeply musing
As we stand before the altar;
The Act of Consecration of Man
Grows into a divining of the Spirit;
The veil of the soul spreads
Before the gaze of the eye of the spirit,
All becomes still before the eye of the spirit.
There can be heard in the ground of the soul
The working of the World's Father-Ground.
The world-calm around us
Fills with this sounding power
That speaks with promise
Within the hoping heart of man.
Divine Might of Worlds.
YOU Who gleam in the chariot of the Sun,
YOU Who shine in the bow of colour
Spanning the skies:
YOU are speaking in the inner place of the soul.
Yet YOUR speaking
Is no present sounding,
Is future-word, that quietly
Carries into the present.
'Become' it speaks.
And dawning it awakens
The picture of man's becoming
In which God's becoming lies hidden.
God's becoming, which in grace
Would mercifully shelter and redeem our errors
In His own divine soul.
Our heart can sense
The salvation that quickens in promise
In the womb of worlds,
That speaks prophetically

In the inmost soul
Of the Mysteries of the world,
Comforting man,
In dark world-night,
Announcing its work
In the realm of Earth,
It speaks prophetically
In the gleaming of the chariot of the Sun
In the shining of the bow of colour
Spanning the skies.

Advent (Insert after the Creed)

Twilight holds sway
In the bounds of the world.
The gleaming of the chariot of the Sun,
The shining of the bow of colour
Spanning the skies,
They fade into far expanses:
Out of the twilight
There dawns divining,
Sun-chariot-shining,
Colour-bow-gleaming,
Beget themselves anew;
Hail to our divining,
Hail to our hoping,
Hail to the One born of light,
Hail to the One the colours bear
The Eternal, divine-wielding
Word.

Advents Epistel

Sinnend werden unsere Seelen,
Indem wir vor dem Altare stehen;

Die Menchen-Weihe-Handlung

Wird zur Geistes-Ahnung;

Der Seelenschleier legt sich

Vor das Schauen des Gestes-Auges.

Es wird still vor dem Geistes-Auge.

Es wird hörbar in dem Seelengrunde

Das Walten des Welten-Vatergrundes

Die Weltenruhe um uns

Erfüllt sich mit dem hörbaren Walten,

Das verheissend spricht

Im hoffenden Menschenherzen.

Göttliche Weltenmacht,

Die DU glänzest im Sonnenwagen

Die DU leuchtest im Farbenbogen,

Der den Himmel umspannt:

DU sprichst im Seelen-Innern.

Doch DEIN Sprechen

Ist nicht gegnwärti'ges Tönen,

Ist Zukunftswort, das leise

In die Gegenwart sich trägt.

Ein «Werde» spricht es

Und ahnend erweckt es

Das Bild des Menschen-Werdens

In dem Gottes Werden sich birgt.

Gottes-Werden, das in Gnade

Unsere Irrtümer huldvoll

In die eigne göttliche Seele

Elösend bergen will.

Empfinden kann unser Herz,

Das Heil, das im Weltenschoße

Verheißend keimt,

Das im Seelen-Innern

Der Welten-Geheimnisse

Menschen-tröstend

Prophetisch in dunkler Weltennacht

Spricht, kündend sein Wirken

Im Erdenreich.

Wirkend in Erdenreich,
Das prophetisch spricht
Im Glänzen des Sonnenwagens,
Im Leuchten des Farbenbogens,
Der den Himmel imspannt.

[Einfügung nach dem Credo]

Dämmerung waltet
Im Umkreis des Alls
Das Glänzen des Sonnenwagens,
Das Leuchten des Farbenbogens,
Der den Himmel umspannt:
Sie dämmern in die Weiten;
Ahnung wird aus Dämmerung,
Sonnenwagen-Leuchten
Farbenbogen-Glänzen
Erzeugen sich neu;
Heil unserem Ahnen,
Heil unserem Hoffen
Heil dem Lichtgeborenen
Heil dem Farbengetragenen
Ewigen, göttlich-waltenden
Worte.

Advent Imagery

'… from the four winds, from the ends of the earth to the ends of the heavens.' (Mk. 13:27. NIV).

THE Advent Epistle is evocative in mood and may at first even appear a little bewildering. This may be due to the presence of dynamic polarities. For instance, our eyes situated as we know at the periphery of the head look at outer things; our ears hidden within the head register sounds within us. At the beginning of the Advent Epistle both these activities are intensified; a germinal spiritual seeing and a spiritual hearing are addressed.

The 'chariot' and 'bow of colours' hint at the central Western mystical tradition. 'Ezekiel saw a vision [Ezek. 1] and described different beings of the chariot' (Sirach 49:9, Hebrew text). The psalmist pictures Yahweh as the 'Shepherd of Israel … enthroned upon the cherubim' (Ps. 80:1), 'who sets the thick clouds [as] his chariot' (Ps. 104:3). Yahweh rode his chariot from Sinai to the sanctuary (Ps. 68:18); 'God's chariots are myriads, thousands on thousands' (Ps. 68:17) describes the angelic army of God. That which was termed during the time of the second Temple 'matter of the chariot' (the chariot of the Cherubim, or the throne of Yahweh, 1 Chron. 28:18; cf. Rev. 4), is now available to all since Christ entered the holy of holies, as the writer of Hebrews explains. And Paul relates the astonishing fact that He became the new 'mercy seat' (Rom. 3:25; the word translated as 'propitiation' in the AV/ KJV and 'expiation' in the RSV is the same as that translated as 'mercy seat' in Lev. 16:14). This was the lid of the Ark set between the carved figures of two golden cherubim with outstretched wings situated in the holy of holies, the cube-room sanctuary at the heart of the Chosen People. Paul is saying that the heart of the cult has been restored (M. Barker 1991).

Experiences of a far-reaching, even ultimate character begin to unfold in the Advent Epistle. Do we not feel the presence of divine creative activity? We seem to be present in the workshop of the Creator Himself in His ceaseless preparation of the future. Cosmic and celestial images of light[2] arise which seem to lead us above; at the same time, we are led to deep musical listening. The second part of the Epistle begins: 'Let there be …', now translated 'Become …', sounding not from what we call the past but from the future. We seem to be present at our own creation! Can it be that we are being gently helped to get beyond our normal yet hopelessly inadequate spatial concept of time and the merely spatial interpretation of our surroundings? Can it be that we are being invited to participate in our own future becoming? And, far beyond our imagining, God's own future is said to be bound up with our own! Yet at the end of the Bible, we recall, God declares that He will dwell with human beings (Rev. 21:3).

Immediately the truth of our wretched condition is mentioned. In the divine presence, we cannot fail to become aware that we are thoroughly faulty creatures. We are simply off-centre. Our need of healing, however, is also met by unequivocal promise. In the original German, 'heart' (the first mention of the word) is immediately followed by 'salvation'. Deeply comforted (this word becomes a proper name in the Easter Epistle: 'the Comforter'—the earlier meaning of this word was 'Strengthener'), we are redirected by the liturgical words towards our earthly existence. A compressed gospel is contained here. After the apocalyptic Gospel-reading with the admonition to stand firm before the Son of man (Luke 21), the Inserted Prayer speaks of the rebirth of the images of light. HE who was announced as shining in these images and as speaking deep within the soul is felt to be approaching nearer. We hear repeated an echo of the angel's greeting, 'Hail' (Lk. 1:28). Is the Epistle celebrating the first Advent, or the second? We seem to be caught up into a world that includes both Advents, or rather the past, present and future Advents, *three* yet one. This world is that of Christian experience, which has always recognized and re-enacted the eternal acts of the Creator. God's utterance—'Let there be …'—is His WORD or deed that continually sustains life.

The Advent Epistle is written on 44 lines. Psalm 44—the number of the redeemed—appeals to God to 'Arise to be our help! and redeem us for Thy mercy's sake!' (Kay 144).

As earthly creatures we may experience that He—God's Deed is Personal—has come in the flesh, that He is alive and that He is coming again. Yet He is the same Being. *Heil*, translated 'salvation' (Epistle) and 'Hail!' (Inserted Prayer), is also the root of the German words for 'healing', 'blessing' and *'Saviour'*. The German language can suggest more than the English translation can. But beyond this fact, 'Jesus', the Greek word for the Hebrew 'Joshua' means 'Saviour'—in full 'Jehoshua' means 'Yahweh is salvation'. As I take part in the Sacrament that indissolubly links past, present and future in its dramatization of the Advent of the Lord, I sense that my heart is linked to His heart, as He draws all men to Himself (Jn. 12:32), making them whole.

On Good Friday when space and time were reconstituted at the heart of the world when He completely assumed the throne of the earthly plane(s), did *He Himself* become the reborn chariot, and was the bow of colour reborn, too (Gen. 9, Rev. 4:3, Rev. 10:1)? From the throne of the cross, God in His humanity is intent on centring the whole of the human race through all cycles of time. The atonement is the greatest healing Deed ever. According to the latest research the ritual meaning of the Hebrew word *kpr* (atonement) means 'restore, recreate' or 'heal' (M. Barker 1996 [2]). No other conceivable means could enable the human being to 'stand' (Lk. 21:28) amidst the rising tide, the 'roaring and tossing of the sea' (Lk. 21:25. NIV)—cf. Matt. 7:27; the storms picture divine punishment (Job 1:19, Ezek. 13:13-14; Sir. 39:28).

'Our heart' (singular, i.e. humanity's united experience) can feel the salvation because the Mysteries of the world, of God's throne, 'hold sway'. The Inserted Prayer is composed of forty-seven words. Ps. 47 declares that 'God reigns over the nations; God is seated on his holy throne ... for the kings [or 'chariots'] of the earth belong to God' (v. 8f). The Inserted Prayer's four-fold 'Hail!' hints at the four directions, and the two further lines complete the picture of six directions. The sides of the Temple's cube-room, when extended, form the three-dimensional cross.

The metaphysical directions comprise the lower part of the Sephirotic Tree of Life. The actual throne of the cross becomes the Tree of Life itself, God's chariot-throne, completely humanized on the plane of history. God Himself comes to rewrite His Word, identical with Universal Man (R. Guénon 2002), at the centre of this cross, first in Bethlehem, then by the Jordan, and ultimately revealing it physically in old Jerusalem at the centre of the world (J. Michell 1991). 'Our heart' learns to be recentred at the centre, 'reborn' in His Heart, to form a new Bethlehem-grotto, a new Jordan-Baptism, a 'New Jerusalem, the Mother of us all' (Gal. 4:26). This process will continue to the end of the world.

During The Act of Consecration of Man, is He choosing me to ascend to His heavenly, golden chariot, in order that I may join with His heavenly hosts? A Christian text of the second century speaking of rebirth, begins: 'I went up into the light of Truth as into a chariot' (Ode of Solomon 38:1). It is straight and narrow, but it leads to life (Matt. 7:14). God is not degraded, but man is elevated by the Incarnation of His Utterance. 'The shining forth of the divine Shekinah is a voice. The Word is the light' (R.M. Benson). Am I to become a mouthpiece, an instrument to witness in word and deed to the Reappearance of the Creative Word, whose aim is the creating of a new humanity and a new world?

> *Lord, mend or rather make us; one creation*
> *Will not suffice our turn;*
> *Except Thou make us daily, we shall spurn*
> *Our own salvation.*
>
> George Herbert

CHRISTMAS

First Christmas Service (midnight)

Into Earth-night
Into sense-darkness
The light of the Spirit streams
With healing grace
It streams forth to us
When we walk
Freed from the body in the land of spirit-beings
After the heart within us
Has felt it in divining prayer.

Know this:
The Christ has appeared in the realm of Earth,
Behold in Him:
The bringer of healing to earthly man.
Through Him has been revealed:
The Father-Ground of all Being.

Second Christmas Service (early morning)

Father Ground of the World:
Our soul is aware that
The healing Creator-Word draws near;
May His power stream to us in blessing,
That it may touch our speaking lips,
And warm our speech-bearing blood
And strengthen our spirit-devoted willing
Through all cycles of time to be.

Know this:
The Christ has appeared in the realm of Earth,

Behold in Him:
The bringer of healing to earthly man.
Through Him has been revealed:
    The Father-Ground of all Being.

Third Christmas Service (mid-morning)

Christ, the revealing Creator-spirit
Of the Father Ground of the World
Has chosen the earthly body,
Wherein it pleases Him to dwell,
To free mankind
From the vain show of illusion,
To free mankind
From the senses' unworthy craving
In all cycles of time to be.

    Know this:
The Christ has appeared in the realm of Earth,
    Behold in Him:
The bringer of healing to earthly man.
Through Him has been revealed:
    The Father-Ground of all Being.

Third Christmas Service (Insert after the Offertory)
(all Holy Night services)

Father, very Ground of All Being,
In that through the Word, Who lived in the earthly body,
The light of Thy clear shining-power has disclosed itself to our
    beholding in Spirit,
That we may know the Divine
    with our sight
And thereby for the unseen our love may be kindled:
We join

In the song of sacrifice
Of the Angels, Archangels, of the Mights, of the Revealers, of
    the Worlds-Powers, of the World-Guides, of the Thrones, of the
    Cherubim and Seraphim
Which sounds forth, that Thou mayest become manifest.

And so may there sound
Through all courses of time:
Healing is through You.

Weihnachten

Epistel der ersten Weihnachtesweihehandlung (in nocte)

In der Erden-Nacht
In die Sinnen-Finsternis
Strahlet des Geistes
Heilendes Gnadenlicht
Es erstrahlet uns
Wenn wir wandeln
Leibbefreit im Geisterland
Nachdem das Herz in uns
Es gefühlet im ahnenden Gebete
    Erkennet es:
Der Christus ist im Erdenreich erschienen,
    Schauet in ihm:
Der Heilbrigner der Erdenmenschen
Durch ihn ist offenbar worden:
Der Vatergrund alles Seins.

Epistel der zweiten Weihnachtsweihehandlung (in aurora)

Väterlicher Weltengrund:
Unsere Seele
Erfühlet das Nahen

Des heilenden Schöpferwortes;
Segnend erströme uns seine Kraft,
Auf dass es berühre unsere sprechende Lippe,
Und erwärme unser sprachetragendes Blut
Und erstarke unser geistergebenes Wollen
Durch alle künftigen Zeitenbreise
Erkennet es:
Der Christus ist im Erdenreich erschienen,
Schauet in ihm:
Den Heilbringer der Erdenmenschen
Durch ihn ist offenbar worden:
Der Vatergrund alles Seins.

Epistel der dritten Weihnachtsweihehandlung (in die)

Christus, des väterlichen Weltengrundes
Offenbarender Schöpfergeist
Hat den Erdenleib erkoren,
In dem er wohnen mag.
Zu lösen den Menschen
Von trügendem Scheinlicht,
Zu lösen den Menschen
Von würdeloser Sinnensucht
In allen künftigen Zeitenkreisen.
Erkennet es:
Der Christus ist im Erdenreich erschienen,
Schauet in ihm:
Den Heilbringer der Erdenmenschen
Durch ihn ist offenbar worden:
Der Vatergrund alles Seins.

(Einfügung in der dritten Weihnachtsweihehandlung nach der Opferung)

Väterlicher Urgrnd alles Seins
Indem durch das Wort, das im Erdenleib gelebt

Unserem geistigen Schauen das Licht Deiner klaren Leuchtkraft such
  erschlossen hat,
Auf das wir das Göttliche
Sichtbalich erkennen
Und dadurch für das Unsichtbare unsere Leibe sich entzünde:

Stimmen wir ein
In den Opftersang
Der Engel, Erzengel, der Urkräfte, der Offenbarer,
der Weltenkräfte, der Weltenlenker,
der Throne, der Cherubine nd Seraphine

Der ertönt, auf dass Du offenbar werdest;
Und durch alle Zeitenläufe
Ertöne es: heilwikendes ist durch Dich.

Christmas Speech

*'God is in heaven, and you are on earth: so
let your words be few.'* (Eccles. 5:2)

THE darkness of midnight, shortly after the turning-point of
mid-winter (in the Northern Hemisphere), becomes a parable for the darkness of a fallen sensory world. This darkness contrasts with the light from another world, the spirit-world. The
call of this uncreated light has nothing to do with escapism. We
are told about the place to which we go every night, and indeed
after death, too, for restoration. In fact, the gracious, healing light
announced at Christmas refers to our essential being. Through
no credit of our own we accustom ourselves to the environment
of our spiritual homeland: 'We are citizens of heaven' (Phil. 3:20.
NIV). The feeling heart of faith prepares the way already in this
world. A mutual influence flows between the realms of the day
and of the night, for in reality the world is one whole. 'In the very
world, which is the world / Of all of us,' wrote Wordsworth, '...
We find our happiness, or not at all' (*The Prelude*, Bk XI).

Faith, one of Christianity's new words but one not specifically
used in the seasonal Epistles, can become again one of the most
wonderful words in human language. 'Divining prayer', including what is technically called 'mental prayer' or meditation, is a
term for the practice of faith. The whole of life is eventually to
become a prayer (1 Thess. 5:17). In Scripture, faith is opposed not
to reason but to sight: 'Only faith can guarantee the blessings that
we hope for or prove the existence of the realities that at present
remain unseen' (Heb. 11:1. JB). 'We live by faith, not sight' (2 Cor.
5:7. NIV). Paul maintains that faith energizes, works, by love.
Faith, he remarks, is born 'out of hearing'; do we not hear both
melody and message in its awakening 'through a word (*rhema*)
of Christ [Himself]' (Rom. 10:17)? To Paul, a developed faith sees
with a NEW sight, new knowledge (Eph. 4:13). We pray in the
Christmas Epistle for the birth of the light in this dark world

that we may truly see and love. Paul's admonition to 'walk by the spirit' (Gal. 5:16-25) takes on more than a merely moralistic significance in the light of the rhythms of life mentioned above. The Christmas Epistle's *'Leibbefreit'*, 'freed from the body', must mean free of 'the flesh', as Paul explains. The Lord has the power to 'form this humbled body of ours anew, moulding it into the image of his glorified body' (Phil. 3:21 KV). 'It will then be purer than the unspotted firmament, brighter than the lustre of the stars; and, which exceeds all parallel, which comprehends all perfection, "like unto his glorious body" ... which He wears in His heavenly kingdom' (John Wesley). Christian faith is walking with a Person; it implies a Way. 'No poet or painter or musician lives more by faith than the man of outward virtue,' claims George Matheson (1842-1906), because the voice is unearthly; it is heard within. 'This is the Way; walk in it!' (Isa. 30:21); the person who does so is 'blessed', 'happy', or 'fortunate' (Pss. 1:1 and 119:1f). But now 'the Way' is Himself (Jn. 14:6). On the way to Emmaus, 'Jesus Himself drew near' (Lk. 24:15) 'as they walked' (Mk. 16:12). 'The Way', the original name for Christianity (Acts 9:2), is rebirth; it is real fellowship. S.T. Coleridge, who possessed a seminal mind, defines faith as 'fidelity to our own being'—which, he insists, is entirely super-sensual. 'Faith subsists in the *synthesis* of the Reason'—for Coleridge, the Logos—'and the individual Will' (*Essay on Faith*). Bishop Butler, in his *Analogy of Religion* (formerly an obligatory study-text for theological students) argues for the word 'probability' as a guide to life; this term, after all, is a synonym for 'faith'. That which 'overcomes the world', John sums up, is 'our faith' (1 Jn. 5:4).

A further step in the Christmas revelation is taken in the Epistle of the second celebration (at dawn). The healing, creative Word is approaching nearer. There is no hint of anything abstractly symbolic or sentimental. Quite practical preparation for renewing the human being concentrates on the most human creative activity. It proceeds in three stages. Like Isaiah during his vision in the Temple (Isa. 6), we pray that our lips may be touched in blessing; secondly, that our blood as vehicle for speech may be warmed, no doubt with interest and enthusiasm (as opposed to obscure passions); and thirdly, that our devoted soul shall be strengthened. All this, for all time.

How can our blood bear 'speech'? The solidity of the body is largely illusory; we consist of over 60% water! Our first drink, our mother's milk, is transformed blood (though for that matter so are finger nails and hair!). Families and tribes are united by blood. In the body, blood is the main fluid, carrying oxygen to every member, repairing, nourishing, renewing. 'Blood', too, is a word for our emotions and passions: it can, as we know, become 'hot', 'cold', even 'bad'. Our blood enables self-experience to unfold. This is the concept of personality—a unit of developing consciousness. Interestingly, even after a blood transfusion we still need to make our own blood. Language, as we know, is essential for all human development. Unless surrounded by human speech, it is said that a baby will die. Is it perhaps more true to say that we live by the word that mysteriously contains, expresses and reflects our personality, than by the blood which bears it? The truth seems to be contained in the expressions 'out of his mouth went a two-edged sword' (Rev. 1:16), and 'sword of the spirit, which is the word of God' (Eph. 6:17); iron is essential in the whole connection of our blood, our speech and our personality—the highest category we know.

For the old sacrificial system 'the life of the flesh is in the blood ... the blood makes atonement by reason of the life' (Lev. 17:11); without the shedding of blood, reconciliation was not achieved. The animal's blood, its life, was a substitute for the human being. 'The Hebrew for burnt offering is *olah*, probably that which goes up'; and the word for the burning is the word used for the burning incense, *katar* (indeed it supplies the word for incense itself *ketoreth*), not the word used for burning to destroy (*saraph*). The offering is not destroyed but transformed, sublimated, etherealized, so that it can ascend in smoke to the heaven above, the dwelling-place of God' (F.C.N. Hicks). When the Creator-Word became flesh and blood, that Blood, the manifestation of burning 'enthusiasm for humanity' (J.R. Seeley, *Ecce Homo*), was sacrificially shed. It became sublimated, etherealized by the fire of supreme *love* —not by that of supreme hate, which was also manifest and thereby met in conflict. The living enthusiasm triumphed, and ever remains. The separation—which is sin, ultimately leading to death (Rom. 6:23)—that had developed into opposition has been undercut. This etherealized Blood CAN be transfused, or rather infused. Every Christian knows Whose Blood flows in his or her veins.

In the Christmas Epistle of the third celebration, the reference to the choice of the earthly body no doubt includes a reference to Jesus. At the same time 'the earthly body' also means the body of the Earth planet. Our own bodies are certainly included too, in so far as they, like that of Jesus (Jn. 2:21), may become dwellings for the Spirit. Paul confirms, 'Don't you know that you yourselves are God's temple and that God's Spirit lives in you?' (1 Cor. 3:16). The body of Jesus; the body of the Earth; our own bodies, all three. The Epistle points to the path towards freedom between illusion and, well, crudity. A faith in the supersensory can now aspire to vision because Christ—a title, meaning 'God's anointed One'—has appeared in the flesh, vindicating the true anthropomorphism. He came not only that we might recognize God, but ourselves 'become divine' (Athanasius). We need neither a sleep of narcotics nor an annihilation through asceticism, not fear or hate, but Reality that fulfils, completely (1 Thess. 5:23).

The season of the Holy Nights is not in the first place a Jesus-Festival, but a Christ-Mass. The Epistles describe the spiritual process. The three Epistles of the three Christmas services are all composed of nine lines. Eight, the number of harmony, complete in itself, is superseded by nine, the number of new beginnings; cf. the nine Beatitudes; the Lord's Prayer; Matthew's Gospel throughout is ninefold (Chr. Rau 1976). The triune progression is also shown in the number of words of the Epistles: a total of 99 (30, 36, 33 = 99, average 33, and all multiples of three). At Christmas we experience the birth of the inner light as a continuing renewal of our spirit. We relate once again to its source, and at the same time are referred to the spirit's far destiny. We realize, too, that we are not alone; we are all members of a progressing humanity. This experience lies behind our wish to communicate at this time of year with friends and loved ones, sending our news, messages, and gifts quite regardless of spatial distance. At this season of goodwill, we open our hearts to the needs of strangers, too. All our little offerings add up to one mighty lyrical outburst. Love towards the human future spills over our customary reserves and barriers. The song of Love overflows to reach out to the largely unconscious, invisible side of our being and through that of outer nature as well. It begins to interest the world of those spiritual beings, the entire nine hierarchies, who already cooperate in realizing the divine plans.

The names of the nine hierarchies comprise the ninth line of the twelve comprising the Christmas Inserted Prayer. Twelve is the number of divine truth working in the Heavens and in the Earth, the number of the building of the body of Christ, the God-man. Something of the Trinity lies behind each of the four triads of lines of the Inserted Prayer. We can sense, moreover, the presence of the four beasts, or living creatures (Rev. 4:6-8), who continually praise God. The numbers of words for each triad are 23 + 16 = 39, and 23 + 17 = 40, making 79 words in total. Psalm 79 brings us down to Earth! It speaks of the temple defiled, of God's habitation laid waste: 'Help us, O God of our salvation, for the glory of Thy Name' (v. 9), i.e. God's self-giving revelation. In depicting the Bethlehem scene, most Old Masters have painted a ruined stable and inn. We are strongly reminded that the human bodily condition still cries out for redemption, for the Incarnation. The original creation was mere finger-work (Ps. 8:3); for the world's salvation, however, God has to 'lay bare his holy arm' (Isa. 52:10). We note that the tenth octave psalm should be of renewed life: 'Hear us, O Shepherd God Israel ... enthroned between the cherubim, shine forth ... come and save us' (Ps. 80:1-2).

The Christmas message is the archetypal gospel: God *has* revealed Himself on Earth for the redemption, the salvation of the race and thereby the whole of creation. The ritual words (24 words, written as 6 lines) are spoken facing 'the faithful'. God's deed of revelation is His Utterance, His Word. The revelation is final and complete. It is unconditional Love. The ancient ritual meaning of the Hebrew *kpr* (atonement) is 'restore, recreate' or 'heal'. The ancient rite of healing harmonizing Heaven and Earth was annually renewed (M. Barker). Christ, by living through the symbolism, achieved a permanent atonement with the Father-Ground of 'all being'. Its remembrance or its re-enacting is a daily celebration of the redeemed community of all lands and ages. 'Mankind knowing and fulfilling its destiny', is F.J.A. Hort's definition of the Church. The earthly act at the altar is at the same time an event 'in the heavenlies', to use Paul's phrase in Ephesians. Our ultimate destiny as the future tenth hierarchy is glimpsed. Was not Augustine right when he pointed out that 'that which is on the altar is the Mystery of yourselves; receive the Mystery of yourselves' (Sermon LVII)?

EPIPHANY

From the bounds of worlds
Has the Star of Grace appeared
To add warmth of heart
To spirit-enlightenment
In the being of man.
Into the light of grace,
Into the gracious beam
Of the Christ-Star
Our souls,
Devoted to the everlasting Father-will,
Would enter in humility.
May the holy Act of Consecration
Be fulfilled
In the upward glance of the soul
To the star
Which called the angels
To announce
To the wise of the world
The gracious appearance
Of the world's light.
May the light of prayer in our hearts
Meet with yearning
The world's light in the Star of Grace.
And life in Christ
Arise within man
When the spirit-beam of the Star of Grace
Reaches the eye of the soul.

Epiphany (Insert after the Creed)

[facing the congregation:]
The world of spirit

Star-radiant
Announced
To seeking human souls
The right way of salvation;
May human souls
Radiant with heart's love
Find the guide on the way:
The World-Star of grace
In the warm
Shining of divine salvation.

Epiphanias-Epistel

Aus den Weltenweien
Erschien der Gnaden-Stern
Zu Fügen Herz-Erwärmung
Zur Geist-Erleuchtung
Im Menschenesen.
In das Gnaden-Licht
In des Christus-Sternes
Begnadenden Strahl
Möchten unsere Seelen
Ergeben dem ew'gen Vaterwillen
In Demut treten.
Vollbracht sei
Die heil'ge Weihe-Handlung
Im Seelen-Aufblick
Zu dem Sterne
Der die Engel rief
Zu künden
Den Welt-Weisen
Des Welten-Lichtes
Gnade-Erscheinung.
Unser's Gebetes Herzenslicht
Treffe sehnsüchtig
Des Gnadesternes Weltenlicht.

Und Leben im Christus
Erstehe im Mensche-Innern
Wenn ins Seelen-Auge drint
Des Gnadesternes Geistes-Strahl.

[Einfügung nach dem Credo]

Es kündigten die Geistes-Welten
Sternstrahlend
Den suchenden
Menschenseelen
Des Heiles rechten Weg;
Es mögen finden die Menschen-Seelen
Herz-Liebe-strahlend
Den Weg-weisenden
Welten-Gnade-Stern
Im göttlich-warmen
Heiles-Leuchten.

Epiphany Ascent

*'For the grace of God has dawned (*epephanê*) upon the world with healing for all mankind.'* (Titus 2:11 REB)

'We have seen His star.' (Matt. 2:2)

THE second time the rite, The Act of Consecration of Man, refers to itself (Advent contained the first) occurs at Epiphany. Most people understand that at Epiphany (from *epiphainein*, 'to manifest') we celebrate the showing-forth of God. The Epistle for Advent (lit. 'go towards') spoke of a divining; the Christmas Epistle (from Christmas Day, 25 Dec., to 5 Jan.) of spiritual vision—this already contains a theophany, an epiphany of the Word. What does the Epiphany Epistle add? With the celebration of the ritual (beginning from January 6th, the last Holy Night), it relates how the eyes of the soul look up, that they are to penetrate towards the gift of the Star. This is no ordinary star. It calls 'the angels' to take the message to 'the wise of the world' of the appearance of God's free gift. 'The wise' does not need to be limited to the Three Initiate-Kings of old. In the Apocalypse, for example, 'the Spirit' (Christ) sends messages (epistles) to 'the angels of the churches'.

This Star shines with a spiritual beam of cosmic light. The term 'cosmic light' grows to become the Solar Christ at St John's Tide (cf. Mal. 4:2, Luke 1:78, Rev. 1:16). But at Epiphany it is the 'Christ-Star' (cf. Num. 24:17), approaching from cosmic widths. Even astronomy recognizes stars are 'suns' though physically distant. E.W. Bullinger (1895) claims the new star was seen at the zenith in the constellation of Virgo-Coma. At Christmas we hear the first use of the title 'Christ' in the Epistles. It appears again in the Epiphany Epistle as the aim of the prayer—we yearn for life in Him. The title 'Christ' (meaning 'God's anointed One', the Priest-King) occurs again in the Easter Epistle, the Inserted Prayers for Ascension Tide, Pentecost and St John's Tide, and the Michaelmas Epistle.

The 'Christ-Star' adds heart-warmth to human spiritual enlightenment. There was an abundance of intellectual and spiritual wisdom in the world before Christ appeared on the Earth. He adds Personality, richly warm, gentle (Michaelmas Epistle) yet mighty (Ascension Tide Inserted Prayer). The light of our praying hearts reaches out, yearning for the Personal light of grace, which is moral perfection, Love itself. A meeting of two streams of spiritual light is indicated (from the Star and from our devoted hearts); a loving union is initiated. Life with Christ within the seeking human being is a developing dialogue of ever more intimate exchange. A correspondence is seen in the fact that children grow down (from the head—Heaven) as well as up (from the feet—Earth). Interpenetrating mutual influence (recognized as the productive 'law of polarity') is the inner pattern of incarnation, and indeed of all productivity. One day, revelation and supplication will be united in total communion. It is a profound biblical conviction that the 'new-Heaven-and-new-Earth' is the counterpart in the universe to Nature, of the new birth in the human heart (2 Pet. 1:19).

January 6th, the traditional date of Jesus' birth, is still celebrated on this day in the Eastern Church. It is also the date of the Baptism in the Jordan. No mention of the Three Kings. We in the West relate the gospel (Matt. 2) to the Epiphany Epistle. But is the Baptism present too? With the use of the title 'Christ', we might expect a reference to the beginning of the three-year's ministry.

The event of the Baptism was the offering of a human being 'to be the vehicle of the Christ' (the Creed). Oscar Cullmann thinks that 'Jesus is baptized in view of his death', pointing out that Mk. 10:39 & Lk. 12:50 show that for Jesus 'to be baptized' means the same as 'to die'. Facing death, Jesus speaks of returning to the 'Father' (Jn. 17). For the writer of the Gospel of Philip, the Baptism in the Jordan already involved a death *before* the death on Golgotha: 'Those who say that the LORD died first and [then] rose are in error for He rose up first and [then[died' (The Gospel of Philip, 56). This 'rose up first' refers to the Baptism as an ascent, a total communion, a death-and-rebirth experience

(Barker 1996). This is the virgin birth, according to the evange-lists (Mk. 1:11, Matt. 3:17, Lk. 9:35, Jn. 1:32-34, 2 Pet. 1:17), the re-creation which also affects us (Eph. 1:6, Col. 1:13).

In Christian origins, martyrdom (Rev. 6:9), resurrection (Ezek. 37:14: the gift of the Spirit transforms) and atonement (healing) add up to apotheosis. First, John speaks of birth from above and seeing the kingdom (Jn. 3); Peter of being born anew (1 Pet. 1:23) and entering the royal priesthood (1 Pet. 2:9). Now Paul adapts an established pattern and speaks of dying with Christ, being crucified and buried (Rom. 6:4-6) in order to rise with Him at a future date. Stripping off the old nature and putting on the new (Col. 3:10) or putting on the new nature created after the likeness of God (Eph. 4:24; cf. Gal. 3:27) originally referred to the mystic's experience of being robed with glory before the throne, putting off the flesh and becoming an angel (M. Barker 1996). The Epiph-any Epistle only appears to omit details of an ascent. Upon closer inspection, it may be heard as a Baptism ascent and rebirth. Is this interpretation justified?

The mood of the Epiphany Epistle is entirely inward; the starry world is nocturnal, inward, divine. The Epistle is written in twenty-seven lines. This is regarded as a significant number in mysticism. 'The Cube of Three [3^3] fully symbolizes the perfect fruition of Divine life' (R.M. Benson). In content and structure, the Inserted Prayer's eleven lines (5 + 6) reveal the hierogamic, or sacred, marriage of Earth and Heaven. The Star's beam is the 'celestial ray', or 'divine ray', of various traditions, i.e. the ver-tical axis, or *axis-mundi*, the 'Way', or 'Will of Heaven'. George Matheson calls it the 'one orbitless star'. Our souls are described as devoted to the Father's eternal will ('Your will' of the Lord's Prayer). But how far do we approach the example of Jesus? He entered the Jordan in humility, following the call to obedience (Matt. 3:15). This is the basic Christian virtue (Matt. 5:3); 'humil-ity' is another name for the truth about ourselves. Jesus trod the complete ladder of humility (Phil. 2:5-11, Heb. 5:8). The human being is indeed the lord of creation (Ps. 8:6). But the expected King-Messiah appeared in history quite unexpectedly as the Suffering Servant (Lk. 4:16-22). The Voice from heaven uniquely quotes two passages of Scripture. 'Certainly, there could be no truer index to Jesus's life than a combination of Ps. 2:7 with Isaiah 42:1f—the Son of God as King and the Servant of the Lord—and this combination, if we go on the evidence, dates from the high hour when Jesus entered on His public work' (J. Denney).

In Temple imagery, the river flowing from the Throne is a river of fire, the barrier between Heaven and Earth. We already anticipate that the heart-warmth will be revealed as flames, but these are the flames of love (Pentecost Inserted Prayer). As into a river, we would 'enter' the gift-star's beam. To do that catharsis is essential; we have to strip off the old creaturely nature. Immediately, the Epistle names the sacred Act of Consecration. We put our trust in the way of the Cross, of offering.

Jesus straightaway met the real test, however, in His threefold Temptation. The test on the three planes (which are metaphysical) was met first inwardly (stones and bread—below; kingdoms of the world—the widths; tempting God—above); the physical cross of three dimensions later erected on Calvary revealed that earlier inner triumph (K. Bittleston; E. Francis). 'The Cross was He and He the Cross,' Charles Williams affirms. He Himself is the Tree of Life. The Star identifies with our mortality (cf. Gal. 5:24).

Mark says He was with the wild beasts and that angels were His servants. This is ascent imagery (cf. Rev. 4); the priests of the Temple were 'angels' (Heb. 'messengers'). The Baptist is 'the voice' (Isa. 40:3), God's messenger or 'angel', too, who announces the need to change to the wise of the world (i.e. not the spiritually wise; cf. 1 Cor. 1:25, 3:19). The worldly-wise include the dry intellectuals, soldiers, tax-collectors, and criminal types (Matt. 3:5, 7, Lk. 3:12, 14), elsewhere called 'sinners', including fallen women. To these people, Jesus preaches the coming of the Kingdom, which is 'among you' (Lk. 17:21. NJB). Its members are to leave the world for the sake of the world. Christ ('God's anointed') is the King born for His people; the Epiphany Epistle declares that our inner life with Him can *begin* (cf. 2 Pet. 1:19). To the predominant language of *Light,* and the birth of that inner *Life,* the Inserted Prayer mentions the streaming of the heart's *Love.* Life, Light and Love are names for the stages of higher consciousness, keywords in John's Gospel. Moreover, the best modern commentary on the Epiphany Epistle may be T.S. Eliot's 'Little Gidding IV & V', concluding *Four Quartets*. Rudolf Steiner commented that 'In the Baptism in the Jordan ... the Resurrection was already given' (Christiania, 10 June 1912. GA 137).

That which is already inwardly experienced is seen on the historical plane in the sacred Blood flowing from the Cross in the greatest deed of Love ever performed. That which inspires our as-yet-feeble answering love is the unimaginable cost of our redemption. It is this, His mission, for which we thank the Father in the St John's-Tide Epistle. For we realize 'there is one body, and one Spirit ... one Lord, one faith, one baptism, one God and Father of all ...' (Eph. 4:5).

We are told of St Jerome that one Christmas night he wished to give a present to the Infant Jesus. First, he offered the Lord his works on the Holy Scriptures, then his labours for the conversion of souls, then such virtues of his as he was able to offer. But all this was not what the Lord wanted. 'Jerome,' He said, 'it is thy sins I wish for. Give them to Me that I may pardon them.' 'The hour of a man's pardon,' writes the Church Father Origen, 'is a festival-day for Jesus Christ.' Penitential sorrow is but the beginning. Your sorrow, Christ promises in the Farewell Discourses—rather a misnomer, for they are actually about 'abiding' in Him—shall be turned to joy, and that joy is permanent (Jn. 16:22).

> *Great indeed is the Baptism which is offered you.*
> *It is a ransom to captives;*
> *the remission of offences;*
> *the death of sin;*
> *the regeneration of the soul;*
> *the garment of light;*
> *the holy seal indissoluble;*
> *the chariot of heaven;*
> *the luxury of paradise;*
> *a procuring of the kingdom;*
> *the gift of adoption.*

St Cyril of Jerusalem, *The Procatechesis* [tr. R.H. Church]

PASSION TIDE

(up to the Saturday before Palm Sunday)

O Man,
The place of your heart is empty.
You have lost
The spirit that wakens you,
Longing for the spirit's
   awakening
Wells in the blood within you.
Through the loss of the spirit
   want
Swells in the breath within you –
Mournful awaiting
Is the part of your consciousness.

Holy Week
(from Palm Sunday to Holy Saturday)

O Man,
The place of your heart is burning.
You live in the cold
Spirit-forsaken
house of Earth —
Sorrow trickles
In the blood
within you —
Hope alone
Streams in the breath within you —
From a grave of hope
A ray of grief
Reaches your
gaze.

Passion Tide (Insert after the Creed)
(for all 4 weeks of Passion Tide)

O Spirit
of the worlds afar
And of the Earth near,
Look not on the sting of evil
In the heart
Of earthly man.
Look how his weakness
Has power to tempt —
My self lies
Lamenting on the ground
Raise it, O Spirit
Of the worlds afar
And of the Earth near.

Passions Epistel

O Mensch: es ist leer
die Stätte deines Herzens,
Du hast verloren
Den Geist, der dich wecket
Sehnsucht nach des Geistes
*   Erweckung*
Wellt im Blute dir
Entbehrung durch des Geistes
Verlust
Wogt im Atem dir —
Trauernde Erwartung
Ist deines Bewusstseins
*   Anteil.*

[Einfügung nach dem Credo]

(Auch in der Karwoche)

Siehe o Geist
Der Weltenfernen
Und der Erdennähe
Nicht des Bösen
Stackel im Herzen
Des Erdenmenschen
Siehe seiner Schwäche
Versuchende Macht —
Mein Ich liegt
Kagend am Boden
Erhebe es, o Geist
Der Weltenfernen
Und der Erdennähe.

Epistel in der Karwoche

O Mensch, es brennet
die Stätte deines Herzens
Du lebst in dem kalten
Geistverlass'nen
   Erdenhause —
Betrübnis riselt
Dir im Blute
Hoffnung allein
Stömt dir im Atem —
Eines Hoffnungsgrabes
   Trauerstrahl
Dringet in deinen
   Blick.

Passion Tide

'Oh my blacke Soule!' (John Donne)

'OMAN!—O Spirit!' The polarity man-God appears in stark-est contrast with the Passion Tide (Lent) Epistle. No imme-diate mediation is offered. The Spirit, we notice, is described as embracing the worlds afar and the Earth near. In this extreme polar situation, if we could achieve access to the Spirit on Earth, an eventual solution to the question of mediation might be found.

'O Man!'—who is addressed? In the first instance, you and I gathered around the altar. But no less real is the wider circle of those included in the Offertory, 'all true Christians ..., those who have died'. As we lower our blinkers, we realize that basically what we colloquially call the whole 'perishing human race' is addressed in the words from the altar. The drastic words of Passion Tide could be said to belong to our whole civilized age, all year round. 'What a wretched man I am!' (Rom. 7:24. NJB). When all is said and done, is the resurrected Life—'Behold I make all things new!' (Rev. 21:5)—taken as the basis of our cultural, commercial, and personal lives? Christ's warnings given to the representative Churches (Rev. 1-4), and in particular that to the angel of the community in Sardis (Rev. 3:1-6), are meant to be taken to heart.

The struggle has intensified today. Precisely in the Passion Tide Epistle we meet the generic term *Mensch*, translated 'man'. This is the etymologically correct term for the correspondence on the one hand with 'spirit', 'the divine' or 'deity', and on the other hand with 'nature'. The term 'man' corresponding to 'woman' is another, quite distinct use. The issue here has nothing to do with reactions or fashions. The Passion Tide Epistle asserts that the individual human being can feel his or her responsibility as a member of the human race. To the nominalist, 'the human race' is but a multitude of single human beings. A feeling for the spiritual concept 'humanity' has largely been lost today. Attempts, moreover, to root out this awareness have annexed the most powerful weapon for change, language itself. The gender question clouds the ulterior motive—which is, to dragoon the human spirit. In this respect, the word 'spirit' in the traditional response to the blessing or greeting 'The Lord be with you', is conspicuous by its absence. 'And with thy spirit' has become 'and also with you' in today's revisions. In the light of English understatement, perhaps the loss is not absolute. 'The Lord', after all, is still the subject. The Act of Consecration of Man makes the spiritual activity quite clear, even adding the verb 'may He fill'.

The location of my heart is described as 'empty'—strictly speaking not the heart itself, which has still to be opened and developed. The psalmist knew that fact too, in his prayer for a real human heart. 'a broken and contrite heart, O God, thou wilt not despise' (Ps. 51:17). We know that Nature abhors a vacuum. The 'place', too, is not a spatial nothingness but a spiritual vacuum that is actually teeming ('burning' is the verb used during Holy Week) with 'wicked designs: acts of lust, theft, murder, adultery, greed, malice, deceitful trickery, sensuality [lasciviousness], jealousy [envy], slander, arrogance and reckless folly' (Mk. 7:21). Rightly interpreted, this is a comprehensive list of twelve anti-virtues. Crudity and perversity; impurity and imperfection; weakness and chaos—these lead to 'all kinds of wild imaginations and extravagant passions' (John Wesley). The source of our troubles is within, not in our projections!

Does the 'sting of evil' ('evil' is named for the first time in the Passion Tide Epistle) sum it up? Sin, says Paul, has brought its 'wages', death (1 Cor. 15:56). How did that sting appear to Jesus? '[It] lay to him in the fact that it was the world's effort to kill virtue, to obliterate goodness, to wipe out from the human heart the handwriting of the moral law.' He faced 'the blackest deed of sin ever perpetrated by the sons of men ... to murder purity itself' (G. Matheson).

Does the seer of Patmos summarize our condition, with the image of the raw, festering 'mortal wound' of the seven-headed beast (Rev. 13:3), the persistent inferiority complex we know so well? Ever again I pit my selfish puniness against God's generous gift of enduring life. Spiritually helpless, I lie on my back complaining about life in this earthly house (Ps. 44:26). Most likely what Paul calls the 'earthly house' or 'tent' is meant, which Paul contrasts with 'a house not made with hands, eternal in the heavens' (2 Cor. 5:1). Are we not all divided? We cannot help ourselves. In the view of Jesus, we are all lost sheep (Lk. 15:4).

The descriptions of the human condition in the Passion Tide Epistle are in stark contrast to the signs of the coming spring surrounding us in the Northern Hemisphere at this time of the year. The Epistle speaks of 'sadness', 'longing', 'loss' ... a sleep, too, is implied. Is this simply a sleep of forgetfulness, or rather the sleep of death? The answer may not be apparent at first, for our typical concerns regarding death are all turned on their heads. We are to change our thinking, and death is the ultimate fact of our existence—the 'last enemy' (1 Cor. 15:26). The Spirit sees that the life of those in Sardis (corresponding to ours, evidently a life of material comforts, concerns and pursuits), has only 'the name of being alive'. The Ascended Christ tells them simply, 'You are dead.' They are to 'be watchful and strengthen what remains and is on the point of death' (Rev. 3:1-2). The implied sleep, from which a spiritual awakening is indicated, is the sleep of materialism. Its name, death of the soul, first appears in the Easter Epistle when the experience of true life reveals its opposite. We even put hope into the grave. And what is 'on the point of death'? Why, our little grey cells! Our ordinary thinking! Now we realize that we almost completely missed the mediator, Speech itself, that— or Who, for it is identical with Universal Man—is present in all situations, almost completely unnoticed (cf. Ps. 139:8)!

Is the body a prison from which the lone soul seeks to fly away in escape? Such mysticism, though impressive, is ultimately based on materialism, i.e. the body is 'only' matter. Is not the body actually an instrument to be tuned by and for the soul, the immortal phoenix-bird? A flute cannot sound if it is stopped with sand. The phoenix-soul cannot simply as a natural gift reveal singing, that is, eurythmy—'inner listening' itself—in a body weighed down with matter. How can its heavenly origin become manifest? The problem is not to escape gravity and over-solidification, but to overcome it and learn a priceless lesson thereby. That lesson can only be learnt on the Earth. Symptoms are not the illness itself. The illness is spiritual. The body's healing is achieved through the activity of the Spirit-Word. This involves a fundamental retuning (Heb. 4:12). Our bodies are to 'suffer a sea-change', as Shakespeare's Ariel (*The Tempest* Act I; Scene 2) describes 'the resurrection of the body, in terms of the body' (Owen Barfield).

A storybook character Baron Münchhausen lifts himself out of the bog by his own pigtail. But the life of the arts provides a less defiant, more reliable method. Scientist and artist pursue complementary paths. The pursuit that researches and reveals the divine in the physical world is science (truth). The pursuit that seeks to raise the physical so that it appears as a 'cloak of the divine' is art (beauty) (R. Steiner, the first lecture, Vienna, 9 Nov. 1888). Both paths play their part in religious life, which seeks the divine everywhere. The Master went before and left beacons. When He rose, His Life, the perfect work of art, rose with Him (H. Scott Holland). His Life, Light and Love pours without interruption from those beacons within and between us, encouraging and actually enabling us even to 'strip off the body of flesh' (Col. 2:11) to reveal the Spirit, His Spirit, for the sake of our fellows and for the whole of creation.

It is worth mentioning that the word 'sin' ('lawlessness', 1 Jn. 3:4) is not heard in any of the liturgical Epistles. However, words about healing, grace or salvation, heard from Advent onwards, certainly imply our separated condition. They lead up to a mention of 'guilt' ('*Schuld*', debt), necessary when the etheric, 'guiltless spheres' come into view at St John's Tide. One little word, appearing here for the first time in the Epistles, proves that these considerations are not merely psychological. That word is *Ich*, 'I' (well translated here as 'self'). 'My self' is discovered in its isolation. This self is not an appendage, a 'thing', but my whole sick, stubborn being. 'The most unbearable punishment for the human soul,' wrote Pascal, 'is to live with itself and think of itself.' It is 'a focusing point where nothing is focused' (William Temple)—the inside of a curled-up wood shaving. The word occurs again only in the Easter Epistle ('the self'), where its isolation, that is, humanity's apostasy here, is overcome. Apostasy is overcome because the sinless one 'was made sin for us' (2 Cor. 5:21) that we can live a really new life. 'True,' wrote Paul, 'I am living, here and now, this mortal life; but my real life is the faith I have in the Son of God, who loved me, and gave himself for me' (Gal. 2:20. KV—'me' here is unique in the New Testament). Christ even identified with the possessed. 'To heal the possessed He had to put Himself in [their] place ... It was wisdom trying to picture the path of folly; it was the calmness of implicit trust seeking to figure the terrors of a shattered brain' (G. Matheson). 'I lay in dust life's glory dead,' sings Matheson in his deservedly famous hymn 'O Love that wilt not let me go', but like St Paul he also clearly points to the 'Cross that liftest up my head'—this can only mean the vertical, heavenly, axis—and the new life arising from that sacrificial life which blooms by shedding itself.

Scott Holland

'Christ's sacrifice is no far-away fact to be shown and gazed upon,' claims Henry Scott Holland (photo: left). 'It draws us also into itself' (*Logic and Life*). Michael Ramsey[3] ascribes a supreme place to this astonishing sermon 'Christ the Justification of a Suffering World'. His remark here could surely also include the four following, passionately intense sermons on sacrifice (given in 1879). Christ took upon Himself the whole agony of man, turning 'death itself into the instrument of the higher inheritance'.

The physiological details appearing in most of the seasonal Epistles reveal how the specifically Christian practice is concerned with biological change. Without it, religion is hardly religion, but rather a moral code or a philosophy, metaphysical or otherwise. To say this implies nothing derogatory about such spiritual disciplines. On the contrary, the sacramental principle, 'the dependence of the higher on the lower' (W. Temple) that summarizes our existence, is an acknowledged philosophical view. That apart, the process of trying to ennoble our human existence is simply a positive way of describing the well-known daily struggle. The Church sacraments, specific channels that develop this insight of dependence, aim to consecrate the whole of human life. These deeds do not monopolize the influence of Christ's grace. Yet the sacraments directly stem from the life of Christ, which—or rather Who—is the perfect Sacrament (O.C. Quick).

The flow of our breathing and the pulse of the blood are manifestations of our life-processes, and they imply the others, like digestion. In such spiritual-physiological details, the Epistles complete our usual notions about ourselves by revealing the corresponding spiritual facts. Our bodies need spiritual renewal. Christ redeemed the human body first by uniting with (not simply visiting) every cell of one particular body (Jn. 1:14). He bound Himself to humanity in a marriage-pact. Such language is not unknown in the Old Testament (Hos. 2:2-5) and is frequently and most profoundly used throughout the New Testament. Even washing of the feet formed part of a Jewish wedding ceremony; 'Jesus washes His disciple's feet to make them worthy successors of the true Israel, the bride of God' (J.A. Findlay). Jesus said, 'I have eagerly desired to eat this Passover with you' (Lk. 22:15; the Passover regarded as God's 'marriage' to Israel) in a New Covenant, or pledge. The first body was remade in the fire of love. That same body, now transformed into a body of light, rose and is offered for the life of the world. The body of mineral-stone became living bread from heaven through love, not magic, 'Take, eat'. He will not rest until all our bodies are redeemed. He will have His creation restored completely (cf. 1 Thess. 5:23). We are married to Another (Rom. 7:4), members of His body, one flesh (Eph. 5:25-32). The poet (G.M. Hopkins) saw the ultimate metamorphosis:

> *In a flash, at a trumpet's crash,*
> *I am all at once what Christ is, | since he was what I am, and*
> *This Jack, joke, poor potsherd, | patch, matchwood, immortal diamond,*
> *Is immortal diamond.*

Human existence *without* what Paul calls 'a spiritual body', that is, in some state of suspended animation, is a fate we hardly dare imagine.

Can He lift us higher than by setting up His own Temple within us? Can He love us more than by vouchsafing to become the food of His own creatures? (John Tauler)

EASTER

The grave is empty
The heart is full
Warmth changes
The beat of the heart
Into rejoicing
Healing power.
The stir of thy blood
Is fulfilment,
The swell of thy breath
Is comfort of Spirit.
The comforter of thy Earth-existence
Walks in the spirit
Before you.

In the centre:

My heart praises
The spirit of God,
My spirit feels
The vanquisher of Death,
Fulness of joy is the streaming power
Of my breath,
Grace is the living might
Of my blood.

Facing the congregation:

Your word go forth
Spirit-wakened
From your mouth.
Christ has risen unto you
As the meaning of the Earth.

Easter (Insert after the Creed)

The airy regions
Of the Earth
Rejoice exceedingly.
The breath of the Earth
Lives in the spirit-radiant
Power of the Sun.
Christ has invaded
Man's
Rejoicing
Pulse of life.
Man finds
In the delight
Of his devout soul:
What has risen in power
From the chains of death;
What in the light has been newborn
In the life of Christ;
What heals the self
In the depths of the soul.
The soul
Which was dead, lives.
The self
Which was dark, shines.
The spirit
Which was close, abounds.
The grave of the soul
Opens;
The grave of the soul
Becomes an altar;
Christ offers
At the altar of the soul
In the spirit-light of man,
To the worlds afar
To the Earth near,
Now and beyond all cycles of time.

Oster-Epistel

Das Grab ist leer
Das Herz ist voll
Wärme wandelt
Des Herzens Schlag
In frohlockende
Heilende Kraft
Deines Blutes Weben
Ist Erfüllung
Deines Atems Wogen
Ist Geistestrost.
Der Tröster deines Erdenseins
Wandelt im Geiste
Vor dir.
Es lobet mein Herz
Den Gottesgeist
Es fühlet mein Geist
Den Todbesieger
Jubel ist meines Atems
Strömende Kraft
Gnade ist meines Blutes
Lebenige Macht. –
Tuning to face the congregation

Euer Wort dringe
Geist-erweckt
Aus eurem Munde
Cristus ist euch
Als Erdensinn erstanden.

[Einfügung nach dem Credo]

Es frohlocket
In Wonne
Der Kreis der Erdenluft
Es lebt

In geistesleuchtender

Sonnenkraft

Der Erde Atem\Cristus ist eingezogen

In des Menschen

Frohlockenden

Lebenspuls

Der Mensch findet

In der Wonne

Seiner hingebenden Seele:

Was in Kraft erstanden

Aus Todesketten

Was im Lichte neugeboren

In Christi Leben

Was heilet das Ich

In den Seelengründen.

Es lebt die Seele,

die tot war

Es leuchtet das Ich

das finster war

Es kraftet der Geist

der verschlossen war.

Es öffnet sich

der Seele Grab

Christus opfert

Am Seelen-Altar

Im Menschen-Geisteslicht

Den Weltenfernen

Der Erdennähe

Jetzt und nach allen Zeitenkreisen.

Easter

'The word is very nigh thee, even in thy heart and in thy mouth.'
(Deut. 30:14)

THE glorious Easter Epistle opens with expressions of symphonic stature. The contrasts between empty and full, dark, and light are dramatically the most extreme. We are there with the disciples and the women at the empty tomb, and then in the Upper Room. Of course, the rhythmic, pulsing life-processes of heart and lung are affected! The glorified Body 'with all the senses and faculties ... communicates itself as a transforming principle to our bodily nature, bringing into us all the joy of the eternal life of God' (R.M. Benson). The spiritual cause of all this healing and joy is Personal. It is named, first, the Comforter. In English, the word 'comforter' with the Latin root *fort* originally meant 'strengthener'. It is normally used for the Third Person of the Trinity, sent by the Father and the Son: 'He will glorify Me, for He will take of what is Mine and declare it to you' (Jn. 16:14). The Comforter leads humanity, spiritually walking this Earth. For Him there is distinction between the two realms but no division; in reality Earth and spirit comprise one world.

The possibility for our walking in the spirit was glimpsed already in the Christmas midnight hour. But during Passion Tide we contracted into the empty earthly house. Death alone is our common lot. By uniting with our ultimate fate, 'He draws all men to himself' (Jn. 12:32). The Easter event restores the walking, but now in the expanded context of our entire earthly existence. The earthly house is now completely inhabited. The second name that is given Him is 'the Vanquisher of Death' (not, for example, 'evader'). The Johannine Christ calls Himself the Door, or Gate of the sheepfold, and the Good Shepherd, too; 'because I lay down my life in order to take it up again' (Jn. 10:17). Sister Death assumes His features, as St Francis knew; we walk in and out through Him Who goes before us—complete, comprehensive Life itself (Rom. 14:9).

The rhythms of the thoughts and of the actual words used in the Easter Epistle build up a tremendous paean. Here a marriage of form and content creates an artistic whole that perfectly serves the spirit's revelation. This is true of all the liturgical Epistles. The subject of number symbolism, an integral part of the way biblical writers thought, re-emerges in the Epistles. For example, one or two links between certain seasons are made concrete through the number of lines. Ascension Tide and Pentecost are linked in this way (both Epistles composed of 20 lines, and Inserted Prayers 17 lines). The five Epistles and Inserted Prayers from Passion Tide to the Easter Inserted Prayer are each composed of 13 lines. Here the link not only emphasizes that there are two indivisible aspects to the Easter event, but the correspondences of the lines themselves proclaim many things. Thirteen is well known as the biblical number of rebellion *and* redemption.

The Easter Epistle, through the very fact that it describes normal earthly phenomena, thereby achieves cosmic proportions. The Mystery of Easter, central to Christianity, is contained in its very method. Here we can directly meet the challenge of 'the life of Christ' with the word 'life' itself. To what such words as 'life' and 'rhythm' refer may certainly be described but have never been defined. Rhythmical details, expressed in the language of number, consequently appear 'suspect' to sceptical people, but are well-known to artists, particularly musicians. A positivist view only admits the prose content of language; all 'poetry' is regarded as unreal; metaphors are 'lies'. Certainly, the musical subject of rhythm initially appeals more as an art than as a science. Yet the Easter-riddle in particular appeals to our reason! Let's look at some specific details.

The harmony expressed by number is widely accepted as basic for sacred architecture. The evidence that Bach and Shakespeare were inspired—in the spiritually-technical sense—by number is irrefutable. And religious texts? K.F. Althoff writes profoundly on the Lord's Prayer, including much that is influenced by numerical research; Christoph Rau reveals rhythms in Matthew and John. There appears to be little justification for persistent uneasiness with the subject of rhythms.

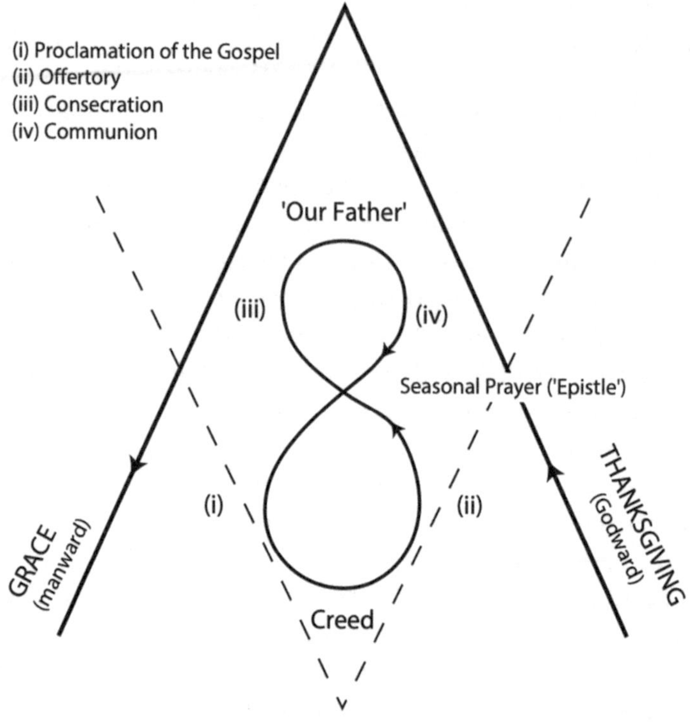

An attempt to show the musical structure of The Act of Consecration of Man (the contemporary form of the Western rite) of The Christian Community. The fourfold lemniscate pattern depicting the movement of the liturgical book (the word and the action at the altar) is a Tree of Life. In the full celebration, seasonally appropriate music is played and sung at the crossing point, which is also the beginning and ending of the service, and instrumental music is also played after the insertions (the Creed and the Lord's Prayer). The crossing point depicts the 'eternal present': it is the point of departure. 'The Epistles' are a new development in the history of liturgy. The lambda figure (continuous lines) = experience of the congregation; the inverted lambda (lines of dashes) = 'onlooker' consciousness, superseded in and by communion (Alan Stott, 1976/95/98).

What evidence exists that literary and musical artists work consciously in this way today? We now know, for instance, that what is called the magic of number, belonging to the central, Western esoteric tradition, was the daily bread of artists like Bach[4] and Shakespeare. Ancient sacred tradition increasingly becomes present artistic life. The true mystics are 'really the precursors of a practical faith' (G. Matheson). Moreover, they are rediscovered specifically as the forerunners of our modern artists. The worship of the Temple—leaving aside the alchemical, scientific aspect—epitomized in the Psalms, is reborn as the musical and recitative arts. Despite the attempted denials, a living tradition cannot be gainsaid. Speaking to the workmen constructing the Goetheanum, Rudolf Steiner referred to gematria, or number mysticism ($a = 1, b = 2$, and so on), as 'super-earthly'. He relates it to the sixth grade of initiation, the Sun-hero, or *Sun human being* (Dornach, 8 March 1924. GA 353). It would seem, rightly pursued, that gematria is a Michaelic study. As we shall see, it even appears as if Michael—who, at the opposite time of year in the autumn, or the fall, leads us to see ever more in Christ's Easter Deed—has set his signature to the Easter Epistle.

Today, the individual's artistic experience, and indeed that of the community too, is a practical spiritual pathway that can be demonstrated up to a point. With the subject of artistic 'appreciation', the conventional distinction between art and science becomes blurred because, like life itself, it tends to supersede both. As we approach the supreme community-building experience of the liturgy, do we need to remind ourselves that 'a greater than Solomon is here' (Matt. 12:42 and Lk. 11:31)? To the question of its source, we shall see that The Act of Consecration of Man is both directly, and in less obvious ways, self-referring. Michael always invites us higher because the Risen Life is inexhaustible. As we are invited to participate in the present Life of our Redeemer, we remember that 'an unintellectual salvation means an unsaved intellect' (Ronald Knox).

An advance precisely in religious understanding will supersede the initial division between art and science. Here philosopher and theologian meet. Rudolf Steiner concludes his self-confessed artistic creation *The Philosophy of Freedom* ('all true philosophers were *artists in the realm of concepts*'—Preface to the first edition 1894, emphases original) which culminates the age of philosophy that began in Greece: 'To live in reality, filled with the content of thought, is at the same time to live in God' (Chapter 15, sentence 64, at the Golden Section of this chapter consisting of 102 sentences). And Augustine ends the first paragraph of his masterpiece, the *Confessions*: '[Y]ou have made us for Yourself, and our heart is restless until it rests in you.' The philosopher and theologian, William Temple (1881-1944, photo: below) points out, begins questioning at the periphery and makes for the centre; the theologian works from the centre towards the periphery.

William Temple

Some selected details may help to show the clarity, precision and scope of the Easter Epistle, and how it incorporates that which it proclaims. Philosopher and mystic can meet:

(i) The liturgical words spoken at the centre of the altar (written in eight lines, the number of resurrection in the New Testament: 1 Pet. 2:20, 2 Pet. 3:5) express four main activities (four is the number of the Earth): my heart praises, my spirit feels, my breath rejoices in strength, my blood experiences the living might of grace. The four clauses, a chiasm, form a hidden cross, a b b a (a = heart praises, and blood experiences; b = spirit feels, and breath rejoices).

(ii) The first-person pronoun 'my' is used uniquely here in the Epistles but without a trace of egoism: the Easter experience, though individual, is shared. Christ paradoxically was always talking about Himself, 'was always saying I, I, I, but He always means You, You, You' (G.A. Studdert Kennedy). Similarly, the meaning of the pronoun 'my' here includes 'His', and, consequently, it means 'our'.

(iii) Death is mentioned here for the first time in the Epistles (to reappear at a distance in the Ascension Epistle), but not abstractly and then only retrospectively. It is mentioned because it is overcome, personally, by death's Vanquisher. The words that follow are addressed to the congregation. Our actual speech shall be awakened from its sleep of death (materialism) by the Spirit. Here 'Christ' (the third name used, the eighth word of this announcement from the altar) shall live. The Inserted Prayer shows how this shall take place.

The Inserted Prayer continues using the third-person form ('it' and 'he'). We noted above the only occasion for the use of 'my'. Throughout there are no verbs in the first person ('I' or 'we'). However, 'the I' as a noun (which, not quite English, is consequently adequately translated as 'the self'), used but once before in the Passion Tide Epistle, reappears here twice in one of the several triads. The word does not appear again in any of the following seasonal Epistles. The Easter Inserted Prayer is composed of 101 words, the numerical equivalent of the names Jah Elohim, Malachi ('messenger'), and Michael ('Who is like God?'). 101 is quite a signature indeed! Ps. 101, 'the psalm of the Perfect Man, identified in act with the Law of the Lord' (R.M. Benson), begins: 'I will sing of your love and justice; to you, O Yahweh, I will sing praise'. The psalmist's heart is 'blameless'. The inner life makes melody to the Lord.

An Inserted Prayer is heard before the Proclamation of the Gospel at Easter. After five words of rubrics (directions to the celebrant), thirteen words in five lines are spoken 'to the faithful' (of our present-day civilization, called in spiritual science the fifth post-Atlantean cultural epoch, when the pentagram became an important symbol for the human being). This manner of speaking from the altar links to the Christmas proclamation (after 13 words of rubrics, 24 spoken words [= 3 x 8, connected to the very special number for JESOUS in Greek, I = 10, H = 8, Σ = 200, O = 70, Y = 400, Σ = 200, total 888, i.e. three eights] in 6 lines), and of Epiphany too (11 lines; 5 + 6 speak of the sacred marriage of Earth and Heaven). The words at Christmas still breathe the air of Heaven, where the four creatures (Rev. 4), each with six wings (4 x 6 = 24), continually say or sing words of praise, the threefold 'Sanctus' (sixteen Greek words; 2 x 8 = an intensified regeneration). Then there are thirteen corresponding words at Easter. The whole Prayer consists of thirteen lines, as do each of the Prayers for Passion Tide. This number (cf. Ps. 13) speaks of rebellion *and* redemption. The final nine lines of the Michaelmas Epistle conclude the process (corresponding to the nine lines of the three

Christmas Prayers). In the only passage in the Epistles of direct speech from the spiritual world (with the exception of the one word *ein 'Werde'*—'Let there be ...'—beginning the second half of the Advent Epistle), the Michaelmas Epistle (41 lines) concludes with a hidden reference to humanity's recreated Temple of heavenly light. Nine is the number of the Godhead; Michael's nine lines of forty-one words about the significance of the Easter Deed link to Ps. 41 with its Messianic references. Jesus applied v. 13 to himself (Jn. 13:18). Messiah appeared as the One poor and needy; Ps. 41, ending the first, 'Davidic' book of the five books comprising the Psalter, concludes in the Hebrew with a doxology consisting of nine words of praise.

The triadic principle is one musical law of the Easter Inserted Prayer's construction. We take one or two examples. The word comprised of eight letters, '*Christus*—Christ', used previously only in the Christmas and Epiphany Epistles, and the eighth word of the thirteen words of the Epistle spoken facing the congregation—appears here three more times. It is first used to introduce the third phrase (line 8, seventeenth word = 10 + 7, beginning with the 88th letter of the Prayer). Its appearance effects a change to the predominantly iambic, rising, rhythm—in both German and English. Thereby it emphasizes the fact which it announces: He 'has invaded man's rejoicing pulse of life'. John wrote that the Word lived (literally, 'pitched his tent') among us (Jn. 1:14). 'It is an invasion from without,' comments William Temple (1917). 'And yet what thus breaks in is itself the power which had always been in control. It was not an alien principle coming into the world but precisely He by whom the world was made and apart from whom, as St John with emphasis declares, there has not even one thing happened.' The idea of grafting in the description 'I am the True Vine' (Jn. 15) expresses it another way.

Human beings can find Christ. Here we hear the second use of the word, line 18, 45th word. Psalm 45 (3 x 15—fifteen is the special number of Jah, and a scriptural number for Christ) depicts 'God the Son coming forth from heaven in divine beauty to assume our humanity in holy wedlock' (R.M. Benson). Christ is discovered, having 'moved in' (*einziehen* is also used with this more homely meaning) into our religious bliss, or ecstasy. Marriage language is used of the divine Lover, of the greatest marriage-event ever. This is not allegory, but reality. The two uses of *Wonne* in the Inserted Prayer are translated as 'exceedingly', qualifying 'rejoice', and as 'delight'. This spiritual delight is experienced in the reborn light of the resurrected Life that arises from death's chains. Those chains are mentioned again in the Michaelmas Epistle, referring there to the dogged attempt of the adversary to enslave mankind.

In the depths of the soul 'the self' is healed, gaining new, shining life and strength. At the expected third use of the word 'self', there appears instead the word 'spirit'. Our existence as self-conscious spiritual beings fundamentally dates its birth from the historical event of the Resurrection. The turned head of the Resurrection Lamb pictures spiritual self-consciousness, q.v. the Ravenna mosaics. Something of the Christ's birth-process (Rom. 1:4) actually lights up in the movement of the Inserted Prayer. Artistically felt analysis should serve the process of Christian self-consciousness, or inner spiritual awakening. Easter is our birthday.

The third moment in the next triad brings the third mention of the word 'Christ' (line 31, 87th word; cf. Ps. 87, concerning renewal through the sevenfold Spirit, speaks of the heavenly Jerusalem; all her inhabitants are born anew). The opening grave of the soul becomes an altar (mentioned for the first time in the Epistles). And now, with the rhythm emphasizing the word, we hear that Christ is the celebrant; *opfert*—'offers'—is the 88th word. (Ps. 88, rather than the 'most despairing' Psalm, prays in the mood of Gethsemane with utter fervour 'speak[ing] of the overthrow of the powers of death without which [the regenerative] life of the Spirit could not be obtained'—Benson 1901, I: 217).[5] Christ offers on 'the Mediatorial Altar of His Divine Personality, that Incarnate Personality which is the true altar' (Benson 1901, II. 198). He celebrates from within humanity (Heb. 7:25; Rom. 8:24), in the cooperating light of the human spirit (i.e. within an adequate consciousness: in the Easter prayers, notice how important are the uses of that little word 'in'!), to the far worlds and to the present Earth (which echoes the appeal of the Passion Tide Epistle). The expression is primarily temporal, not astrophysical. Christ, our Great High Priest (Heb. 4:14), whose offering was complete, is now working even beyond the end of time: 'I make all things new' (Rev. 21:5). We heard of the 'Song of Sacrifice' at Christmas, but here with the creation of the human altar, we witness the first, or rather the eternal, deed of offering. The phrase 'deed of offering' itself comes to the fore in the Pentecost Epistle, bringing for us an increased sense of responsibility.

Here, as a final climax to the final six lines, the emphasized word 'Now!' is heard. In the German, the same line contains the letters A and Z ('*nach allen Zeitenkreisen*'; actually A and Z first appeared as the 84th and 104th letters embracing the words '*Christus ist*': 4 points to the earth; 8 to resurrection; 10 is ordinal completion pointing to moral perfection). The last line here corresponds to the last line of both the Michaelmas Epistle and Inserted Prayer. The word 'Now!' introduces a specific focus not found in any other Epistle than these two. Easter and Michaelmas are seasons of transition, human festivals celebrated just after the spring and autumn equinoxes in nature. Both festivals in different ways are characterized by a strong call to consciousness. The colours of the vestments show this: the strong colours of Easter are reflected in the delicate, more inward colours of Michaelmas. In the musical circle of fifths (the keys), glorious C-major and its relative A-minor (the minor keys keep more in the shadows) of Easter, stand opposite the subtle change and the inner threshold from sharps to flats (F#/G♭-majors; D#/E♭-minors) of Michaelmas. In a lemniscate diagram of the year, both festivals occur at the crossing point, the heart of the year. This is also the moment of our entrance and exit to every celebration, as we cross from daily or weekly life to face and thereby recreate the altar: 'Let us worthily fulfil …', crossing ourselves therewith in the ever-renewed dedication of consciousness, 'Now'. 'Now is the day of salvation', Paul insists (2 Cor. 6:2).

Thrasybulos Georgiades (1907-1977) writes perceptively about the spiritual importance of the present moment, the 'Now'.

Speaking of the forte climax in the passage in Mozart's *The Magic Flute* where, prior to the initiation trials, Sarastro for the last time sings *'die Stunde schlägt'* ('the hour strikes'; No. 19, b. 63), he writes: 'Awareness of the Now, and thus of the action, becomes visible as fire and power that scorches and blasts everything. It is like a flash of lightning revealing Substance itself, which the sudden illumination that Meaning, as it were Eternity, is manifested as the Now, as unique moment' (tr. A.S.). The stage directions ('A thunderclap; fire flashes from the door; a loud chord') merely support what the music has already created. We are reminded of the meteorological phenomena accompanying the theophany on Sinai (Ex. 19), of the New Testament interiorizing at Pentecost (Acts 2), as well as the activity proceeding from the throne in Heaven (Rev. 4:5). What are called the Synoptic Gospels report that the Son of man comes in the eternal present 'as lightning that comes from the east [and] is visible even in the west' (Matt. 24:27

Agnus Dei, the Easter Lamb with a cross-bearing nimbus and with the cross and banner of the Resurrection—in a reflective gesture of complete self-knowledge. Outstanding 12th century roof boss; Quire, Canterbury Cathedral, UK.

and Lk. 17:24). The Song of Songs, in its one mention of the name of God, likens love to the fire of God (8:6. RV 'flame of the LORD', Heb. 'flames of Jah'), that is, warmth manifests as lightning; God manifests His love, His eternal Word.

It is not the written word, not even the Word hidden in Sacraments, but the Word manifest in our persons which must convert the world … The shining forth of the divine Shekinah is a voice. The Word is the light. We have not to speak about Him merely. He must be speaking in us, and then, whithersoever the word goeth, it will accomplish the will of the Father in the power of the Holy Spirit [R.M. Benson, letter to Father O'Neill, 4 Aug. 1876].

ASCENSION

Father-Ground Divine
Wielding among all beings
Thou hast sent HIM
And He has confirmed Your sending
Through His word, His passion,
Through death and the conquest of death.
He lives in earthly being
Transfiguring earthly
With heavenly being;
We behold with the
Visionary power of our hearts
His elevation to the heavenly
For the sake of the earthly being.
May He abide with us
In that He abides with Thee.
With His power in our souls
We would fulfil The Act of Consecration
Looking up to HIM.

Ascension (Insert after Creed)

Christ's power of soul
Reveals itself
In the heights,
Into which He embodies
Earthly being.
The eyes of our soul
Behold Him
In the realm of the clouds
Bestowing blessing
On earthly being.
Therefore our hearts

Praise and magnify Him
And our song of praise
Shall follow His course,
That we may be
Confessors unto Him
Through all cycles of time.

Himmelfahrts-Epistel

Göttlicher Vatergrund,
Der DU waltest
Unter allen Wesen:
Du hast IHM gesandt,
Und Er hat Seine Sendung bekräftigt.
Durch Lehre, Leiden
Durch Tod und Todes-Sieg;
Er lebet m Erdensein,
Verklärend das Erdensein
Mit Himmelssein;
Wir schauen mit Herzensseherkraft
Seine Erhöhung
Zum Himmelssein für ds Erdensein.
Er wohne bei uns,
Indem Er wohnet bei Dir.
Mit Seiner Kraft
In unseren Seelen
Wollen wir verrichten
Die Weihe-Handlung
Aufblickend zu IHM.

[Einfügung nach dem Credo]

Es offenbaret sich
Christi Seelenkraft
In den Höhen,
Denen Er einverleibt

Das Erdensein.
Unsere Seelenaugen
Schauen Ihn
Im Wolkensein
Segen spendend
Dem Erdensein.
Darob lobpreisen Ihn
Unsere Herzen
Und unser Preisgesang
Folge Seinen Spuren,
Auf das wir seien
Die sich zu Ihm bekennen
Durch alle Zeitenkreise.

Ascension

'While he was blessing them, he parted from them and
was taken up into heaven.' (Lk. 24:51)

ASCENSION DAY is celebrated forty days after Easter Sunday (Acts 1:3), which is always a Thursday (Thor-day, or Jupiter Day). The Ascension completes the Resurrection process that crowns the earthly life of Christ. Towards it He looked, as He set His face towards Jerusalem (Lk. 9:51, the assumption is the Ascension). In rejoining the spiritual realm, the King's Son (Matt. 22:2; cf. 25:34) takes His renewed manhood with Him. Humanity is present in the Godhead for all times to come. 'Crowned with glory and honour' (Heb. 2:9), He takes up His eternal reign. We can sense the great joy experienced in the world of the nine heavenly hierarchies as He passes them (a day for each one, up to Pentecost Sunday), having completed His mission. Christian art has often pictured a physically ascending figure leaving a group of disciples on the Earth looking heavenward. In Luke's account, 'a cloud took him from their sight'. 'Two men dressed in white'—which, in the language of the Temple, means 'angels'—ask, 'Men of Galilee, why are you standing here looking up into the sky? This Jesus, who has been taken away from you up into heaven like this, will come again in the same way as you have seen him going into heaven' (Acts 1:9ff. WB). The way from Heaven to Earth, and from Earth to Heaven, is now completely opened up.

The Passion Tide Epistle spoke of 'my self', and the Easter Epistle of 'the self'. Now the Ascension Tide Epistle addresses the Father-Ground and speaks of HIM. Although neither the earthly name nor the cosmic office is used, the sending of the Son, His confirming that sending, and the cardinal events of the life are mentioned. His teaching, His passion, His passing through death and death's overcoming are specifically named. These events do not indicate the bare plot for a play, be it even a Mystery Play, where a *deus ex machina* arrives to save a tragedy. It is not even true to say that God Himself is the main actor. It is not an actor–audience situation at all! Far rather, His life is the reality, the divine manhood, whereas 'All the world's a stage, / And all the men and women merely Players', as Shakespeare's Jaques exclaims. Our lives, beset with illusions, are the imperfect dramas we make them as we stumble about trying out roles, until we learn that 'looking up to Him' we will find the true source of Personality. The reason for this is that He has identified with 'my self' and 'the self' of humanity (Gal. 2:20), by penetrating to the heart and marrow itself (cf. Heb. 4:12). The Redeemer-King, Christ Jesus, the Saviour, comes directly to you and me, bringing the truth in His own Person.

The 'life—death—new-life' triadic summary points to His after-death tableau-experience. This is on quite another level to that of any other human being. The Ascension Tide words are gloriously clear and supremely positive. This soul-tableau of a life devoted to the Father's will is the inexhaustible source of the written gospels and of all inspiration in social development. The fruits of His completely non-egotistical life are His gift of grace to mankind. It is the supreme pattern of all right living. The tremendous achievements of His mission are the very means enabling Him in His present life to perform the task of mediation for us. This death and new life is yours and mine. We are free to accept it, but for freedom to be real, He has to allow that we may reject it, that is, we may reject Him Who is our Higher Self.

His royal life-embracing heavenly and earthly existence is expressed in rhythmically balanced forms. Form and content are perfectly married. Summarizing, we observe that the Ascension tide Epistle (68 words in 20 lines) is formed in two sections (10 + 10 lines; 34 + 34 words). The six lines 8-11 may be heard as a middle section (20 words = 2 x 10). The emerging Trinitarian life (lines 14-15) is expressed in 9 words (3 x 3; we met 3 x 3 x 3 = 27 in the number of lines of the Epiphany Epistle). The total number of words suggest a link to Ps. 68 (used by the whole Western Church on Whitsunday, following the Feast of Weeks of the Jewish Church). It describes the LORD who 'rides on the clouds' (Ps. 68, v. 4. Cf. Dan. 7:13; Matt. 26:64) and whose followers also ride

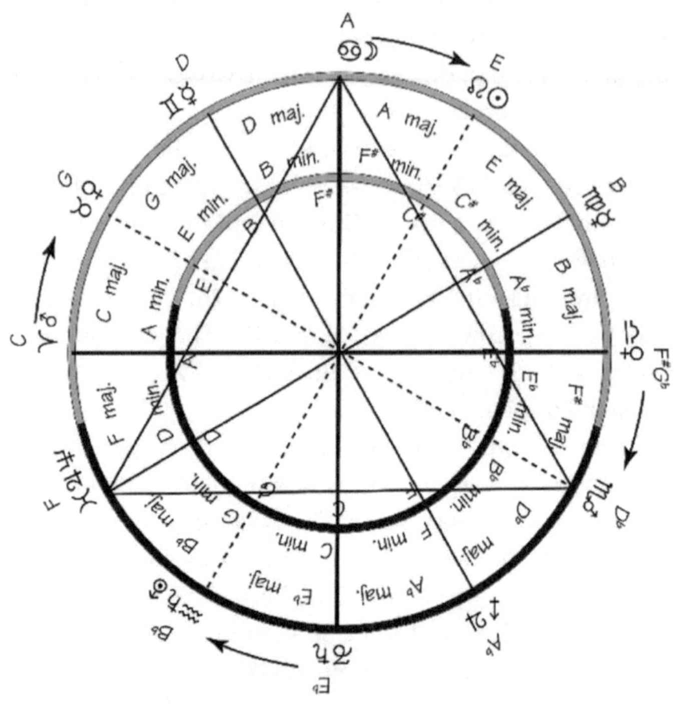

The tone-zodiac of Hermann Beckh (a founder-priest of The Christian Community), first published in 1925. Beckh relates the three 'crosses of the keys' to will, the feelings and thinking (C-major, G-major and D-major crosses) behind which, he shows, one can sense the Father, the Son and the Holy Spirit.

chariots (Ps. 68:17); Paul interprets Ps. 68:18 as foreshadowing the Ascension (Eph. 4:8). (The Beatitudes of Matt. 5 exhibit a similar balanced form in the Greek: 2 x 36 words for each quartet.)

The middle line of the Inserted Prayer, 'bestowing blessing' (*'Segen spendend'*) sums up the Ascended life. The three sentences consist of 13 + 10 + 23 words, naturally forming 10 + 7 lines of 23 + 23 words (in detail: 46 = [13+10] + [10+13 words]). The biblical significance of the numbers and the correspondences with the Psalms are particularly suggestive; 23 is a special number for a special psalm. Seven speaks of spiritual perfection; it is the number of grace, the hallmark of the work of the Holy Spirit. Ten speaks of moral perfection. Seventeen (10 + 7) is the special number of God's Chosen People. Thirteen speaks of rebellion and the need of redemption. All three Passion Tide prayers and two Easter prayers are composed of thirteen lines, which sequentially correspond.

The number 46 links to Ps. 46, which contains the lines 'God is in the midst of her' (v. 5), and 'Be still and know that I am God' (v. 10). At the still centre of the world, it seems, a solid cubit (*anmah* = 46) shone with the glory of the Shekinah, the Divine Presence (Gen. 6:16), indicating transcendent perfection (M. Mahan). Later, the Tabernacle was ten cubits; the cube-room of the Temple twenty cubits; New Jerusalem a cube of 12,000 furlongs = 82 x 33. Incidentally, in the AV, or King James Version (1611), of Psalm 46 (= 2 x 23), the 46th word from the beginning is 'shake' and the 46th from the end is 'spear'. Some scholars ask whether the Bard—William was born and died April 23rd; the First Folio appeared in 1623—had something to do with the AV or KJV, Psalter, perhaps even more. The number 23 is a significant number in esotericism.

'Transfiguring' is a unique term in the liturgical Epistles. The earthly can become translucent, can be raised to the heavenly state, through the channel of His very Deeds themselves. Those selfless Deeds live on. Christ Jesus has completed the entire development which mankind has yet to undergo. He dwells both with the Father and with us at the same time. Wholeness has been restored. The realm of the clouds is mentioned, recalling the cloud of the presence that once surrounded the sanctuary. All creation exists in Him (Col. 1:15). His life is thus the perfect Sacrament. The earthly clouds in the sky are more than a parable since He 'fills the whole creation' (Eph. 1:23). It is fitting that Paul's Letter to the Ephesians suggests itself for commentary, if it is 'the divinest composition of man', as S.T. Coleridge claimed. 'He is not ascended from us but in us,' writes R.M. Benson, 'lifting up His head to breathe, as it were, the pure air of the height of the mountain of God, while His blood circulates in us His members here below.'

The Ascension Tide Inserted Prayer immediately mentions our praise and 'our Song of Praise'. We are there on Olivet, watching. Yet the heart's seership does not rest content with beholding; we must burst into singing. The content of that response, following His path of success, expresses our deepest desire to join all those who by confession belong to Him. Echoes of the traditional *Te Deum*, for example, occur throughout the liturgical Epistles, particularly in the two Festivals that mention singing (Christmas and Ascension Tide); perhaps, too, the triune ending links to St John's Tide with the petition for the eternal blessing of the divine power and love. 'To be able to sing joyfully and confidently about our beliefs is probably a unique Christian achievement. It is difficult to imagine an erudite philosopher, an exotic mystic, a freethinker, agnostic, or atheist, getting up and with full heart setting his beliefs to music. Yet that is exactly what we Christians do Sunday by Sunday, day by day ...' (H.E. Hopkins). The Christian family were first called followers of 'the Way' (Acts 18:26, 19:23, 24:14). He alone is the Way (Jn. 14:6). Peter confessed, 'You have the words of eternal life' (Jn. 6:68); indeed, He *is* eternal life (Jn. 11:25, 14:6). The psalmist's deepest wish is to 'dwell in the house of Yahweh forever' (Ps. 23:6). This looks to the double achievement of the Incarnation, which was 'the climax of immanence in the world' (Illingworth), and which at the same time expressed the eternal, transcendent Word of Life. The Incarnation of the divine Word, God's Deed, was a taking-up of a particular human nature—a fallen creature, despite all the preparation.[6] The whole of creation was represented in that body; the whole of creation is being renewed by that body. The 'temple of His body' (Jn. 2:21), that portion of the spiritual-physical universe He entered, was restored by His uniting with it (Jn. 1:14). This restoration, or recreation, in which the Psalmist wished to live 'forever', is called by the synoptists 'the Kingdom of Heaven' and by John 'eternal life'. After the Ascension, it gradually expanded as He took on the entire Earth planet as His dwelling, to redeem it entirely. The completion of Christ's work of renewal can only occur through human cooperation here on Earth. Wherever we live on the Earth, the celebration at the altar creates harmony, and sends blessing to the whole of creation. It all happens through the mediation of Him who dwells with us, and to Whom we look, literally in the original, 'in the heavenlies' (Eph. 1:3 & 20, 2:6, 3:10).

'We must look forward to the great shout of Hallelujah,' writes Father Benson (1901, II. 342). 'That word is here [Ps. 102:18] intimated for the first time [in the 'Book of Praises']'. 'A new-born people shall praise JAH, shall sing Hallel to JAH.'

Rudolf Steiner's paraphrase, and indications to express the word 'Hallelujah' in eurythmy, unlocks its potential: 'I purify myself from everything that hinders me from beholding the Godhead' (GA 277a. 41).

Psalmus vox ecclesiae, said St Ambrose: 'The Psalter is the voice of the Church.'

PENTECOST

Christ sends
Into our souls
The Spirit of the Father-Ground,
The World-Physician Who heals
The weakness of souls
And the infirmities of mankind.
May the health-bringing Spirit
Wield in the word of offering
Blessing the deed of offering,
That works
In The Act of Consecration,
Which stems
From Christ's ordaining.
And shall come to pass
In the light
Of the Spirit
Who heals
What proves sick
In earthly being.

Pentecost (Insert after Creed)

Behold the flames,
They are the revelation of the Spirit.
So flame the word
Of The Act of Consecration;
So flame the deed
Of The Act of Consecration.
The flames stream heavenward;
They stream forth from human hearts.
Which, filled with Christ,
Kindle their being

In the word of praise,
That is filled with the Spirit
He has summoned,
That human souls,
Healed by the Spirit,
Keep themselves whole
Through all earthly cycles of time.

Pfingst Epistel

Christus sendet
In unsere Seelen
Des Vatergrundes Geist.
Der da heilet
Als der Weltenarzt
Der Seelen Schwachheit
Und der Menschheit Gebreste.
Der Heilbringende Geist
Walte in dem Opferworte
Segnend die Opfertat,
Die da wirket
In der Weihe-Handlung,
Die entstammet
Der Einsetzung Christi,
Die geschehe
In dem Lichte
Des Geistes
Der da heilet,
Was krant sich erweiset
Im Erdensein.

[Einfügung nach dem Credo]

Schauet die Flammen
Sie sind des Geistes Offenbarung.
Es flamme das Wort

Der Weihe-Handlung
Es flamme die Tat
Der Weihe-Handlung
Die Flammen strahlen himmelwärts;
Sie erstrahlen aus Menschenherzen
Die erfüllt von Christus
Ihr Wesen entzünden
Im Lobesworte,
Das erfüllt vom Geiste,
Den Er herangezogen,
Dass Geistgeheilt
Menschen-Seelen
Gesund sich halten
Durch alle Erden-Zeitenkreise.

Pentecost

'The spirit of man is the candle of the LORD.' (Prov. 20:27)

AT Pentecost (known since Thomas à Becket's day as Whitsun, or 'White Sunday'), the Jewish Church celebrated the giving of the Law on Sinai. It also celebrated the first fruits, specifically the first wheat harvest (Ex. 34:22), the last of the cereals to ripen in Israel. It consequently marked the closing of the grain harvest. The Christian Pentecost occurs ten days after Ascension Day.

Phillips Brooks

The Pentecost Epistle invites us to behold the flames which are the Spirit's revelation. Initially, we see the seven candles on the altar, described in the Apocalypse as 'the seven spirits of God', and 'the angels of the seven churches' (Rev. 3:1, 1:20). A burning candle consuming its own substance and converting it into light and warmth, is a picture of the soul-life of the Christian disciple. 'The spirit of man is the candle of the Lord' (Prov. 20:27, cf. Ps. 18:28) inspired a famous sermon by Phillips Brooks (photo: above), author of 'O little town of Bethlehem'—a foremost preacher at the beginning of the present Michael Age beginning in 1879. Then, we remember the first morning of Pentecost, when 'a sound came from heaven like the rush of a mighty wind', the natural emblem of the almighty Spirit; 'and there appeared to them tongues as of fire, distributing themselves and resting on each one of them' (Acts 2:2f). We also recall love's creative fire in the ritual words spoken at the end of Offertory. The writer to the Hebrews calls God 'a consuming fire' (Heb. 12:29, quoting Deut. 4:24) in connection with the altar-offering. For the first sacrifice, God provided the fire (Lev. 9:24), which was then retained in the sanctuary. God provided the fire, too, for Elijah's famous sacrifice in his contest with the priests of Baal (1 Kings 18). The

Epistle goes on to entreat that the words and the deed of The Act of Consecration of Man catch fire. The spiritual enthusiasm of the healthy, undivided human heart is the source of the flames. The Epistle, moreover, recognizes Who causes that fire to stream from the healed or redeemed heart, praying now from within humanity. In a Whitsun-tide letter, R.M. Benson (1824-1915), a master of the spiritual life, claims: 'The Spirit which is given to us is not the power of the Spirit, but the Spirit of power.'

The Inserted Prayer consists of 17 lines, the special number of God's Chosen People in their probation. It is composed of 53 words. (153, mathematically = 9 x 17, expresses God's people in their glory. This triangular number is the number of fishes caught on that morning after the Resurrection; Jn. 21:11.)[7] The heart of the Inserted Prayer is the seven lines from 7 through to 13. Twenty-four beautiful and succinct words speak of the flames streaming heavenwards from hearts lit by the Spirit summoned by Christ—the Name, in connection with human hearts, appears in the central line. Words—and words are deeds—of praise is the Christian life in essence. The Epistle for Pentecost even declares the origin of the ritual. It 'stems from Christ's ordaining'. Not

Duccio di Buoninsegna, The Miraculous Draught of Fishes

74

only do we remember the night He was betrayed and when He commanded: 'Do this', but the ritual celebration that re-enacts, enables Communion with His present life. In partaking of the communion, wrote St Paul, 'you proclaim the Lord's death until He come' (1 Cor. 11:26). Whatever else this is said to mean, He comes forthwith to bestow His present life.

In the New Testament, death is never mentioned without the resurrected life. Initially, we may say that there is one Communion, which is forever renewed. Though Communion is (i) complete here and now, yet we are always learning to participate in experiencing and approaching that completeness. The liturgical Epistles contribute inestimably by leading to an even richer experience of Communion. (ii) The entire Christian year forms a cosmic, yet at the same time homely, complete artistic whole. Cyclic form reappears in music and in countless stories (the archetype of 'there and back again' is the Parable of the Prodigal Son, Luke 15). (iii) Then again, from a third standpoint of Communion, we go on to see that the whole of human life is seeking for consecration. He rays *back* his perfected Manhood from His achievement, which for us is a far-future goal. There is no limit to the free offering of abundant life which satisfies every claim, meets every need. Our life, then, at every stage is guaranteed.

'Christianity is before all things a medical movement,' claims George Matheson (1824-1906), Scotland's blind seer. It aims 'to have the deformed transformed'. Matheson himself lost his outer eyes as a young man but gained a remarkable inner vision that he put to the service of his ministry in spoken and written words. He occasionally even uses the word 'clairvoyance', which the *Oxford English Dictionary* defines as 'deep insight'. Beethoven (1770-1827, photo of his memorial statue: left) lost his outer hearing as a young man but thereby developed a supremely sensitive inner ear. His creations, far ahead of his contemporaries, not only helped to democratize music by making an appeal to humanity at large. The late piano

Beethoven

sonatas and string quartets portray the inner life itself. They point to a different, and even more glorious, Christian musical future, that is, one born out of a new relationship to suffering. This path was fully trod by the Son of man. To partake of the regenerate, ascended life, every disciple is required to confess that which is revealed through Him. Then 'the World-Physician' can work, sent by the Father and the Son. He works on the weakness and infirmities of mankind through every individual who cooperates with Him, here, on Earth, who can say: 'I fill up in my flesh what is still lacking in regard to Christ's afflictions, for the sake of his body, which is the church' (Col. 1:24).

ST JOHN'S TIDE

To the Father-God,
All-wielding,
All-blessing,
Shall stream the devout and
heart-warm thanks of our souls.

Light of worlds, radiant with grace,
Works in ethereal spaces, in fullness, in ripening glory.
The all-wielding power of the Father-God
The all-blessing might of the Father-God;

They work in the flowing ether-light;
They create in the living world of being;
They ripen in the mist of the world;
Into the Sun of Christ that saves mankind.

In the ethereal rays of the Sun-spirit
You, our Deliverer, didst enter
The seed of mankind, laden with guilt, needy of healing
On the field of Earth.

And he who humbly bore
The Father-Spirit
In the sphere around his body —
I o a n e s
He spoke the Word of flame —
Heath-bearing, and conscious of guilt,
The Word of Annunciation.

His word of flame,
prophetic of grace,
Shall burn in our hearts
With longing towards You;

Who hast borne life from death for us guilty mankind,
That we may live
In pure ethereal spheres
Which can bear the guiltless alone
On the glancing waves of Spirit.

He who longs for the light,
Who knows the light,
Reveals to our souls
Radiant grace of light;

May our soul receive
The bestower of light,
The Creator of light,
In life's fullness of love.

St John's Tide (After the Offertory)

Fired by the light of the Sun —
Devoted to the light of worlds —
Thou, who humbly bears
The Father-Spirit
In the sphere around thy body —
    I o a n e s
Herald of salvation,
Behold the deed of the altar
Which blesses human beings,
Which we would fulfil
Through the blessing of Christ,
Who is announced to us
In you.

Johanni Epistel

Zu dem Vatergotte
Dem allwalteden

Dem allsegnenden
Ströme unsrer Seelen
Fromm-ergebener
Herzwarmer Dank

———————————

In Ätherweiten wirket gnadestrahlend
Weltenlicht, in Fülle, in reifendem Glanze
Des Vatergottes allwaltende Kraft
Des Vatergottes allsegnende Macht

Sie wirken im flutenden Ätherlicht
Sie schaffen in lebender Wesenswelt
Sie reifen in der Welten-Mitte
Zur Menschen-erlösenden Christus-Sonne.

In der Sonnengeistes Ätherstrahlen
Zogest Du, unser Erretter
In des Erdenfeldes schuldbeladne
Heilbedürft'ge Menschensaat.

Und der den Vatergeist
Im Umkreis seines Leibes
Demutvoll tragende
    I o a n e s
Er sprach der Verkündigung
Heiltragendes, schuldbewusstes
    Flammenwort

<u>*Sein*</u> *Gnadeahnendes*
    Flammenwort
Es brenne in unsren Herzen
Verlangend nach Dir,
Der Du für uns Menschenschuldner
Das Leben aus dem Tod geboren

Auf dass wir leben
In reinen Äthersphären

Die schuldloses nur tragen können
Auf den erglänzenden Geisteswellen.

Es offenbaret unseren Seelen
Der Licht-ersehende
Der Licht-erkennende
Des Lichtes Gnadenstrahlung;

Es empfange unsere Seele
Den Lichtes-Spender
Den Lichtes-Schöpfer
In Lichtes-Liebe-Sinn.

[Einfügung nach der Opferung]

Sonnenlicht-entflammter
Weltenlicht-ergebener
Du, der den Vatergeist
Im Umkreis seines Leibes
Demutvoll tragender
   I o a n e s
Heiles-Vor-Verkünder
Schaue auf des Altars
Menschensegnende Tat
Die wir vollbringen wollen
Durch Christi Segen
Der uns in Dir
Verkündet ist.

St John's Tide

'His lightning lights up the world.' (Ps. 97:4).

THE Christian year following the life of Christ reaches a climax at Pentecost. In the Calendar of the many (Western) Churches, apart from special Festival Days and Saints Days, the 'weeks after Pentecost' follow until Advent of a new Christian year approaches. This second period of the year, following Pentecost, is devoted to our response to the life of Christ in which we participate during the longer first period (Advent to Pentecost). The renewed liturgy chooses St John's Day (24 June) and Michaelmas Day (29 September) and creates two new Christian Festivals. They are named respectively after a human being and after a spiritual being, and across the year complement respectively Christmas and Easter. St John's Day occurs just after Midsummer Day, as Christmas is celebrated just after the winter solstice. Three festivals from the Father (Advent to Epiphany), three through the Son (Passion Tide to Ascension Tide) are now completed with three to the Spirit (Pentecost to Michaelmas).

Not one Epistle mentions the name Jesus; the only human name mentioned is John the Baptist in the untranslated form 'IOANES' (meaning 'Yahweh is gracious'). In one of His 'Amen-sayings', Christ says, 'among those born of women there has risen no one greater than John the Baptist' (Matt. 11:11 & Lk. 7:28). Can we say that he spiritually represents humanity, carrying out the office of ever announcing the progressive coming of God? John was 'a man sent from God' (Jn. 1:6). Does not the evangelist carry this name too? And are we not all 'sent from God', sent down into the earthly world, to discover, prepare and reveal its meaning of which the words of the sacrament of Baptism in The Christian Community speak? In this sense, the Baptist stands as the representative disciple of the Lord, the prime example of 'the priesthood of all believers'.

In representing humanity, John represents at the same time the Father Himself, the source of all the creative forces that have formed humanity. Ultimately these come from the spiritual, starry periphery which embraces our existence. In this sense, we identify with John who was the greatest before Christ, beholding that which takes place on the altar and which now brings the inner forces of reconstitution. At midsummer, you and I, children of Adam, identify with, or 'are', John-Everyman preparing for the specific Spirit-child, whose inner birth progresses a little further each midwinter. St John's Tide can only be fully understood in relation to Christmas.

The message (*evangelium*), as the word says, comes from the angels. Perfect ministration, the aspiration of all the professions, is founded upon a kindred, human experience. Jesus, moreover, 'proclaimed that if ministration was to be complete, man must be the angel to man. That is the thought at the root of what is called the Christian ministry' (G. Matheson). Who are 'the little ones' whose 'angels do always behold the face of my Father, who is in heaven' (Matt. 18:10)? Literal children? Rather, argues Matheson, these are sacrificial spirits in humanity who 'have attained to the nature of God … they alone can behold like … still rejected and despised by men' but while yet on Earth, they are privileged to 'behold the face of their Father who is in heaven'.

The main human contribution to the divine world of the Father is simply deepest gratitude. We have been showered with gifts, both in creation (mere finger-work; Ps. 8:3) and in redemption (for which God has to 'bare his holy arm'; Isa. 52:10). One of the greatest gifts of all is that we have been enriched so that, in our turn, we can assist the course of the divine self-giving. We thank the Father, for He is as active in the work of redemption as Christ Himself: 'He did not even spare his own Son, but gave Him up for us all; and must not that gift be accompanied by the gift of all else?' (Rom. 8:32. KV; cf. Gen. 22:16). That 'God so loved the world that He gave …' (Jn. 3:16), 'is the heart of the gospel,' observes William Temple (cf. 1 Jn. 4:10); 'it was an act at a particular time and place', St Bernard says. 'In the first work (Creation)] He gave me myself, in the second (in Christ) Himself; and when He gave Himself, He gave me back myself (Redemption)' (*De Diligendo Deo*). Our usual 'thanks' is raised to an ultimate degree; that which we render becomes spiritual substance. The ritual use of the word shows that the human being is at last learning to bless. The name Eucharist means 'thanksgiving'. Christ blesses the bread, or unites Himself with it, to be the life of the world. Could anything more wonderful ever happen in this world? After the bestowal of the Spirit at Whitsun, we gain in awareness and responsibility. Our response is to render such gratitude that ultimately amounts to a self-bestowal. By endeavouring to give ourselves in this way to the Father, our Maker, we give ourselves to the Earth, our 'first love' (Rev. 2:4). For now, we realize Whose body it is—the Spirit of the Sun, Christ Himself (cf. Ps. 84:11, Rev. 1:16). Giving is always accompanied by a receiving. Its spiritual name is love. 'Faith and love are the beginning and the end of the Christian life,' wrote Clement of Alexandria, 'and neither of them can be taught, though all that comes between them can be taught.'

One matter that 'comes between' here is our consciousness of guilt, or debt (cf. Matt. 6:12—consciousness comes prior to praying for forgiveness). The divine will, the law or bond with all its obligations is clearly against us, approved by our own signature, confessed by our consciences (our hearts). But Paul tells the Colossians, God has cancelled all debts. 'Although you were dead because of your sins and your uncircumcision, He [God] has brought you to life with Christ. For he has forgiven us all our sins; he has cancelled the bond which was outstanding against us with its legal demands; he has set it aside, nailing it to the cross' (Col. 2:14. REB). In this passage, recognized as difficult, several strands come together. If we take the passage in reverse order, we have, regarding sin: (i) the cosmic significance of the sickness of sin has been removed by the Deed of Golgotha; (ii) our personal sins are forgiven, too. The etymology of 'forgive' is 'wipe away', but may we not also say that our own sins are 'for-given' = 'given back'? If so, thank goodness! for now I can do something about the *consequences*. I may assist destiny's Lord in His redemptive work, through learning to take some responsibility for my own destiny. 'The mercy of God is not a mere forgiveness, but it is a raising of the sinner out of his fallen condition' (R.M. Benson).

George Matheson

The reference to circumcision points to the first major crisis of the infant Church. The Messiah came to the Chosen People, who were slow to realize that His Deed was for all peoples (although the psalmists and some of the prophets declared it). Christ initially came to the Jews, certainly, but thereby He entered the seed of humankind. For claiming to forgive sins and for preaching a universal gospel, Jesus was killed. He appeared to be violating the sacred marriage-pact between Yahweh and His Chosen People. 'The life that came forth on Easter morning ... was neither Jewish nor Greek nor Roman. It was a new life from an unprecedented stem—a life even without virgin mother—a life fresh from God' (Geo. Matheson: photo above). Ever since then all talk of a 'chosen race', 'master race', 'superior breed', 'ethnic cleansing', and so on, derives from outdated prejudices. Once-legitimate doctrines are tragically re-manifesting in the world as crude, decadent practices. But I am absolutely included in this; I too must grow beyond unquestioning pride in my origins and root out my unbearable prejudices. The old Adam is to be stripped away.

Politicians, though, are wholly responsible for the pejorative meaning of the word 'nationalist'. A 'united states of the world' is an enforced abstraction; a 'world commonwealth of nations', however, can only be mutually helpful. The solution to our social problems is to become social human beings. This may one day come, for Christ's deed was the seed of a new humanity. Christ, explains St Paul, is the new Adam, the new heavenly Man (1 Cor. 15:45). No wonder John's word burns like a trumpet sound! 'Our God is a consuming fire,' says the writer of Hebrews (12:29, quoting Deut. 4:24. See also Pss. 50:3, 97:3), in connection with offering. In relinquishing separation, 'the kings of the earth' can only gain enrichment.

Today, it is said, a seat is still left for Elijah at the circumcision of every child. The door is left open for the returning Elijah at every Passover celebration, too. But Gabriel announced that John will come 'with the spirit and power of Elijah' to turn human hearts (Lk. 1:17). After the Transfiguration, Jesus confirmed that John was the returning Elijah (Mk. 9:12; Matt. 11:14). Elijah-John calls for a change of thinking, an appeal to return to a lost innocence, a lost participation. Moral zeal for the spiritual implies moral decision (1 Kings 18). Conscience is born within. The 'still small voice' (lit. 'voice of thin silence'; 1 Kings 19:12) is an obscure, ambiguous phrase. Something very strange happened to Elijah. Is it 'the sound of a gentle breeze' (LXX), a 'faint murmuring sound' (REB), a 'soft whisper' (GNB); a natural phenomenon or a theophany, or somehow *both*—if the Logos is poetic, creative, and not simply prosaically defining? The ambiguity of the original should be retained in translation (Prickett 1986). If the spirit of nature has entered the human being, consciousness will change, indeed it *has* changed. Recognition of that change ('self-knowledge') is pressing, for left to themselves things will turn into their opposite—as Shakespeare's tragedies amply prove—naiveté will become tyranny, fair becomes foul. To go for the 'natural' is no longer enough. No wonder Elijah talks to Jesus about his *exodus* (Lk. 9:31; *not* 'decease' AV). The *exodus*, the 'coming out' from Jerusalem, was the beginning and prototype of the return of the human race. The question of relapse or renewal increasingly faces every single individual throughout the whole world. Elijah-John's fiery, moral word lives on. His office, 'baptism of repentance' (Acts 13:24) replacing circumcision, prepares (Acts 19:4) for Christ's baptizing 'with the Holy Spirit and with fire' (Matt. 3:11 and Lk. 3:16). We appeal to John in our deed of offering, our spiritual exodus *in* the world but not *of* the world, yet *for* the world—and starting with myself.

The Advent Epistle speaks of the Chariot of the Sun. The Epiphany Epistle named the Christ-Star's gracious beam. The St John's Tide Epistle now names the Christ-Sun, the Spirit of the Sun. Expressions of living light reach a crescendo. We seem to be surrounded by creative, living light. The phrase 'guiltless spheres' describes the bright spiritual realms which open since our debt to the Father-God has been cancelled. It points to our eventual divine destiny (Ps. 82:6, Jn. 10:34f.). The living ether-light that ripens is Personal. We recall that God created light on the first Day of Creation (Gen. 1:3); some take this to be the begetting of the only Son, God's Utterance, His manifest Word, the Logos Himself. Later God created the Sun and Moon (on the fourth Day: Gen. 1:14-19). The saviour-God not only 'covers himself with light as with a garment' (Ps. 104:2); the Johannine writer declares, 'God is Light' (1 Jn. 1:5). The Sun, seemingly 'out there', is but a picture of God's limitless love that sustains life on Earth.

In any case, we are not told to look far away to behold God's present glory, for He has chosen to dwell with His children. Indeed, He has already manifested His light-glory. In possibly the most astonishing and shocking verse of his gospel—though over-familiar to us—the Johannine writer declares that he saw the manifestation, the glory or Shekinah of God, in the flesh— meaning the whole humanity—'we have beheld his glory, glory as of the [an] only Son from the [a] Father' (Jn. 1:14). His countenance is 'as the Sun shining in its strength' (Rev. 1:16). A very early hymn promises those who awaken from the sleep of death that 'Christ will give you light' (Eph. 5:14). In the recon- stituted, recreated human nature Christ achieved through tak- ing a human life through death, and the subsequent bestowal of the Spirit to the community of believers, a new and bright humanity can already be glimpsed. 'If we walk in the light, as He is in the light, we have fellowship with one another' (1 Jn. 1:7). Like a seed, the Christ-Sun grows and ripens from the spir- itual centre (the heart).

The outer sun will gradually pass away; 'He must increase, but I must decrease' (Jn. 3:30). Historically, the 'increase' began from the Body on the Cross at the heart of the world. 'Is it not from the night that it shines forth?' asks Teilhard de Chardin. 'The light does not merely shine upon the gloom and so dispel it; it is the gloom itself transformed into light,' wrote William Tem- ple. On the Cross, 'the eye of Jesus gleams out with resplendent brightness. It is from the dark room, from the rayless environ- ment, that the Face of Jesus shines. It shines with an unborrowed glory, a glory all its own. Nothing assists it; everything resists it; but it shines, and we see it and are glad' (G. Matheson).

With corrected vision, we may 'see everything as it is, infinite' (Blake). The maturity of Wordsworth's 'Ode, Intimations of Immortality from Recollections of Early Childhood' (composed around his thirty-fifth year) lies not in the poet's bewailing the passing 'splendour in the grass, of glory in the flower', but 'rather find[ing] / Strength in what remains behind ... In the soothing thoughts that spring / Out of human suffering; / In the faith that looks through death, / In years that bring the philosophic mind.' The development of personality, C.G. Jung reminds an audience of teachers, is a task for the second half of life. He concludes his lecture, 'Personality is T A O.'

The ancient T A O-philosophy re-emerges in the West as the universal law of polarity. It can very inadequately be summed up as: growth and form, and the lightning power creating dynamic balance. Polarity is the law of the etheric world. Coleridge found it everywhere from the life of the Trinity to the workings of Nature and of the human mind. (The middle way between two extremes is already presented in the Epistle to the third Christmas service.) The sounds of the name IOANES are related to the T A O of Far-Eastern tradition. As three vowels in the order I A O, we recognize one of the names of God. The initial vowels IOA of IOANES suggest that the human being, as God's creature, reflects his divine origin. Man's response to the divine contributes a new emphasis.

The Bible ends with a vision of the city of the New Jerusalem 'which comes down out of heaven from God'. The imagery for this climax is of bride and bridegroom, which also expresses the polarity man / God. It is the most intimate image possible; God is Love and Life as well as Light. ALL polarities are concluded at the end of the age (cf. Eph. 2:16). The Sun and Moon are no longer apparently 'out there', for 'the glory of God is its light, and its lamp is the Lamb. By its light shall the nations walk; and the kings of the earth shall bring their glory into it' (Rev. 21:2, 23f.). Union with the ardent divine Lover, the Beloved, is pictured not as a state of mind, but as taking place with the redeemed human community. Love in itself, as Emil Brunner says, is simply Life without sin. It implies fellowship as we walk in the Light.

MICHAELMAS

While we should experience in our hearts
In this hour from the altar
The Act of Man's Consecration:
The eyes of our souls behold
The countenance of him, who is himself
The countenance of the God of man.
So stood he once before HIM
who was pleased graciously to send
Christ, the Healer of man
From heights of spirit to depths of Earth.
So stands he in these world-days,
Clear shining, as Christ's countenance
Guardian of the sacrifice of consecration.
Under his feet, easy of the weight of Earth,
He treads the powers that would fetter the Spirit of man
With chains of earthly slavery,
And from human hearts he draws forth
The free power, which can bear the earthly
Into heights of heaven, purging it
And receiving spirit.
Solemnity streams from his shining,
Solemnity that before the gentleness of Christ
Prepares the heart of man for the light.
Whoever beheld him in years past
Perceived the stern hand, stretched out
In menace towards the Dragon's power.
Whoever beholds him today becomes aware
How for a while he changes
The sternness against the power of the enemy:
And forms his hand to beckon
Pointing to man: *'Follow me*
I lead you to higher divining

Of the deed of life and death on Golgotha,
Which working on in earthly man,
Creating into times to come,
Shall to life bring light;
That in the earthly light
The heavenly light vanish not,
Which should lighten as from the beginning,
So now and in all cycles of time.'

Michaelmas (Insert after Creed)

May he who stands before the countenance
Of Him Who passed through Golgotha
For the healing of mankind:
Lead us into the depths of soul,
From which Christ sends His power
Bearing Spirit into human hearts
If, in true longing for salvation
Human beings feel the fire of their hearts
Rightly enkindled.
To him who stood before the Father-God,
Who stands before the Son-God:
To HIM shall our hearts turn,
That the Healing Spirit may work in us,
As from the beginning,
So now and through all cycles of time.

Michaeli Epistel

Unsere Seelenaugen schauen, da wir
In dieser Stunde von dem Altar
Die Handlung der Menschenweihe
Im Herzen erleben sollen:
Das Antlitz dessen, der da ist
Selbst des Menschengotten Antlitz.

So stand er dereinst vor DEM,
Der Christus, den Menschenheiler
Aus Geistes-Höhen in Erdentiefen
Gnadevoll hat senden wollen.
So steht er in diesen Weltentagen
Hellstrahlend als Christi Antlitz
Als Hüter vor dem Weihepfer.
Die Gewalten, die den Menschengeist
In Erdensklaverketten fesseln wollen,
Tritt er unter sene Füße.
Die der Erdenschwere ledig sind.
Und aus Menschenherzen holet er
Die freie Kraft, die Irdisches
In Himmelshöhen läuternd
Und geistempfangend tragen kann.
Aus seinem Schein erstrahlet Ernst,
Ernst, der vor Christi Milde
Das Menschenherz dem Licht bereitet.
Wer ihn schaute noch vor Jahen
Erblickt' die strenge Hand
Drohend nach des Drachen Kraft gestreckt.
Wer ihn heute schaut, wird gewahr
Wie die Strenge gegen Feindgewalt
Er für Augenblicke wandelt:
Und seine Hand zum Wink gestaltet,
Dem Menschen deutet: <u>Folge mir</u>.
Ich füre dich zum höhern Ahnen
Der Lebens-Todestat auf Golgatha.
Die fortwirkend im Erdenmenschen
In Zukunftszeiten schaffend
Dem Leben Licht bringen soll.
Dass im Erdenlichte nicht erlösche
Das Himelslicht, das leuchten sollte
Wie vom Angbeginn, so jetzt
Und in allen Zeitenkreisen.

[Einfügung nach dem Credo]

Der da steht vor dem Antlitz
Dessen, der durch Golgatha
Zu der Menschen Heilung ging:
Er führe uns in die Seelentiefen,
Aus denen Christus seine Kraft
Geisttragend in Menschenherzen
Sendet, wenn Menschen fühlen
In wahrer Heilessehnsucht
Das Herzensfeuer recht entzündet.
Der da stand vor dem Vatergott,
Der da stehet vor dem Sohnesgotte:
Zu IHM sollen wenden sich
Unsere Herzen, dass der heilende Geist
In uns wirke, wie vom Anbeginn,
So jetzt und durch alle Zeitenkreise.

Michaelic Vision

'Let the light of your face shine upon us, O Yahweh.' (Ps. 4:6).

Michael

MICHAELMAS is the concluding Festival of the Christian year as celebrated in The Christian Community, although the final weeks do return to Trinity. The Epistles reach a certain culmination in their references to the ritual itself. The full name, 'The Act of Consecration of Man', is already heard at the beginning of the Advent Epistle. It is called 'the holy Act of Consecration' in the central lines of the Epiphany Epistle. 'The altar of the soul' is born in the Easter Inserted Prayer. 'The Act of Consecration' is the term used in the Epistles for Ascension Tide and Pentecost. The opening words of the Michaelmas Epistle bring together 'our souls', 'the altar', 'the Act of Man's Consecration ... in our hearts'. This impressive description prepares for 'the Countenance' of 'the God of men' (icon above). A climax is reached by calling him 'the Guardian' of the act of sacrifice itself. Rather than the militant figure of the archangel Michael (Rev. 12:7f), following Emil Bock, we recognize him as 'another angel' who swings the censer (mentioned by name in the Old Latin Mass) and celebrates in heaven (Rev. 8:3). Should the two aspects perhaps be combined into the warrior-priest? Is perhaps the battleground the human heart itself, imaged there in the actual altar?

Let us approach an answer by enquiring about 'the countenance'. The culminating experience, the *summum bonum* of human life is the *visio dei*, the vision of God. 'I had heard of thee by the hearing of the ear; / But now mine eye seeth Thee,' Job concludes (Job 42:5f). 'This mystical solution,' comments A.S. Peake, 'is the most precious thing the book [Job] has to offer us.' The sixth Beatitude, 'Blessed are the pure in heart, for they shall see God' (Matt. 5:8) is already implied in the Psalms: 'The upright shall behold his face' (Ps. 11:7; see also Ps. 24). The psalmist, because of his 'integrity'—or, as mystical interpreters claim, because he expresses the mind of Christ—is set 'before Thy face' or 'in Thy presence for ever' (Ps. 41:12). According to Christ of the Gospels, this is the angelic experience too, for the angels of the little ones—probably humble Christians—'always behold the face of my Father who is in heaven' (Matt. 18:10). Paul points to the experience by comparing it with the case of the Israelites in the time of Moses. Moses was constrained to wear a veil to hide the splendour of the spirit, fading as it was. But now, Paul proclaims, we can become that which we love, 'because there is no veil on our faces, the faces of us all reflect the glory of the Lord. We are thus being transformed into his very likeness, always moving on to greater and greater glory—and this is the work of the Lord, who is the Spirit.' For God 'has made His light shine in our hearts to illumine them with the knowledge of the glory of God, seen in the face of Jesus Christ' (2 Cor. 3:18, 4:6. WB). 'Glory' is the manifestation of God; those like Him shall enter His presence, or 'see' Him.

Is this an earthly seeing? Paul apparently never saw Jesus in the flesh. He did meet Him on the road, however, speaking to Him personally in Aramaic (Acts 9:5f). One day, Paul wrote later, we shall not need the veil of nature which reflects like a mirror, but we shall all see directly 'face to face' (1 Cor. 13:12). One who sees beyond the natural face, James adds, is a 'doer of the word' (Jam. 1:22-25). He or she thereby gains 'the perfect law, the law of liberty'. In other words, you 'persevere' in true self-knowledge, eventually to recognize Who is appearing in the depths of your heart. Paul's question 'Who are you, Lord?' received the answer of the Ascended One, 'I am Jesus [Heb. 'Saviour'] whom you are persecuting.' It changed Saul into Paul, the greatest disciple of the Lord, and the first and greatest theologian. What did he see? The Church which he was persecuting was the resurrection body of Jesus. *The appearance on which Paul's whole faith and apostleship was founded was the revelation of the resurrection body of Christ, not as an individual, but as the Christian Community'* (John A.T. Robinson, 1952, italics original; cf. 1 Cor. 8:12, Gal. 4:14, Philem. 17). In his celebrated portraits, Alexander Whyte (1836-1921) says directly:

> He has nowhere else to dwell … [A]s he is the Christ, He dwells in His people and can dwell nowhere else, in heaven or in earth, but in His people.[8]

The name of Christ's regent or countenance, the archangel Michael (the name is not actually spoken in this or any liturgical Epistle) means 'Who is like God.' Is this name an exclamation, a challenge, or both? That depends upon me: I myself have to recognize (confess) the Son of man as the God of men. The name-question is actually our own question, too. The Michaelmas Epistle speaks of Michael's attempts to help us to answer it. In the only direct speech from the spiritual world to be used in the Epistles (apart from 'Let there be …', which, incidentally, is only one word in German: *ein 'Werde'*), Michael tells how he would lead us in freedom. His eloquent gesture is a call to follow him to higher reaches of faith. At the conclusion of the 41 lines, Michael speaks of leading us to further vision of heart-knowledge of the most wonderful deed that ever did or ever will happen on the Earth. His 41 words perfectly answer the situation described in the Passion Tide Epistle, which is also composed of 41 words.

Incidentally, Bach took the gematria of his name extremely seriously. The sum total of the letters of his name in the standard number-alphabet, a = 1, b = 2, and so on, is: 'J.S. Bach' = 41, and 'Bach' = 14. Fourteen is also the gematria of 'David' in Hebrew (*dvd*, which means 'the Beloved'), the 'sweet psalmist of Israel' (2 Sam. 23:1). This phrase in the Hebrew refers to musical execution (W. Robertson-Smith) and should rather read 'the singer of the songs of Israel' (NJB); 2 Sam. 6:5, 14 tells how David danced and played joyfully before the ark 'with all his might'. Bach felt a particular kinship to the divine musician David, and to the calling of a church musician. But beyond this, especially in the last twelve years of his life, he respected the sacred nature of instrumental music itself, with its power to portray and thus reveal divine Mysteries (H. Kluge-Kahn 1985).

Ps. 41 contains Messianic references to the Passion and Crucifixion. In the Johannine writings, the Cross is the very manifestation of the Father's 'glory', that is, unconditional love for humanity, because it completely identifies with humanity. This 'is as much as to say: when Christ was crucified, chaos had come again—and then God repeated His act of creation' (C.H. Dodd). Out of the darkness at the turning point of time (Mk. 15:33), the God Who said, 'Let there be light' and divided the light from the darkness (Gen. 1:2, 3) created afresh. To the newly created Now, He has 'shone in our hearts to make known his glory in the face of Christ' (2 Cor. 4:6. NIV).

Every autumn, or fall, when approaching the culmination of the Christian year, an inner echo of the Easter experience arises across the year within the praying heart. If Golgotha is the death of you and me (Heb. 2:9), who is it, then, that prays? The answer is already in the Psalms, but it usually escapes attention. The Hebrew of Ps. 109:4 says, 'I [am] prayer'. Another 'I am' in the Psalms is 'I am [for] peace' (Ps. 120:7; cf. 1 Cor. 14:33). The war-songs of the Prince of Peace, the words and actions of human beings in the vanguard of a recreated and—through God's grace—a recreating humanity, are sung prayers. Two further 'I am' sayings in the Psalms are 'I am God, your God' (Ps. 50:7), and 'Say to my soul, "I am your deliverance!"' (Ps. 35:3). Humanity is to regain a 'singing-speaking, speaking-singing' which was lost when speech 'fell' into prose (however, a case of 'loss and gain'!).

The Psalter does not simply belong to the Old Testament; it belongs to the New Testament as well. Jesus and the disciples sang psalms (Matt. 26:30), probably Pss. 115-118; Paul advises to sing psalms (Eph. 5:19, Col. 3:16); the liturgical Epistles speak twice to the same effect. This presents a Michaelic challenge today. The prince of the people of Israel (Dan. 10:13, 21), leader of the

Hebrew mission to prepare the body for the Incarnation, surely inspired the composition of the Psalms—the speaking and the singing. 'Prayer, the intimate, personal communication between and "I" and a "Thou" in adoration, petition, confession, and ultimate surrender was born among the Jews' (A. Heidenreich). Some Psalms originate from Solomon's Temple, the whole Psalter representing the hymnbook of the second Temple. 'The religious lyric is the one great artistic achievement of ancient Israel,' claims a leading scholar on the Old Testament, 'and the Book of Psalms is the chief literary monument of that achievement' (H. Wheeler Robinson).

Father Benson, the writer of possibly the most impressive devotional-analytical work on the Psalter, including a splendid translation, claims, 'The whole Psalter, although lyrical in its form as consisting of separate odes, may be regarded as one continuous epic ... belonging to the promised Messiah ... [W]e must always recognize not man but the God-Man' (R.M. Benson 1901). The Psalter reveals the mind of Christ (cf. 2 Sam. 23:2). We note that the Beatitudes (Matt. 5) which contain the heart of His teaching, are all either quotations or echoes from the Psalms; the originality lies in their choice and order. Three of the Seven Words (or sayings) from the Cross, moreover, are from the Psalter. An early tradition tells that on the Cross Christ sang from Ps. 22 through to Ps. 31:6. Further psalms are quoted in the Crucifixion narratives. The Church Fathers seem agreed that 'all the Psalms appertain to the Person of Christ' (Jerome). For no less than twelve centuries, knowing the entire Psalter by heart was a requirement for ordination. How many priests, like Thomas Aquinas, knew, and how many know today, the whole Bible by heart? Certainly, in all Scripture Christ turns His mysterious Countenance towards us. Indeed, all language baptized by the fire of the spirit becomes sacramental (see Thomas à Kempis, *The Imitation* Bk IV, xi, 4). At two different moments in The Act of Consecration of Man, we stand; we align ourselves, that is, to the vertical world-axis, in order to receive Him.

The renewed liturgy speaks of 'the Song of Sacrifice', in connection with love for that which is not visible (Christmas Epistle), and 'the Song of Praise', again in connection with the heart and the eyes of the soul (Ascension Tide Epistle). Inspiration for prayerful songs, it is confirmed, may be found in inner experience. In the culminating vision of the Bible, it is Michael who celebrates the heavenly ritual, bearing a golden censer to mingle incense with 'the prayers of all the saints' (Rev. 8:3f). Dare we, too, look to him in his present, second mission to spiritualize the human body? The atonement, or healing, of the Temple rite, it was said, 'refers to the singing'.[9] The full depth of music's meaning is experience of the Divine: 'My glory / strength and my music is Yah' (Ps. 118:14), joining with the music of all creation (Pss. 98:5-9; 148; 150).[10] This is the essence of the first word carried out in eurythmy, Hallelu-jah, taken from the Psalms (15 of the 150 contain this word) and given a fresh paraphrase-translation by Rudolf Steiner (GA 277a. 41).

15th century medallion depicting Christ as Janus (R. Guénon 1995).

Michaelmas, the grand culmination of the yearly cycle, which began with the eternal begetting of the cosmic WORD, looks to the future, to cosmic DEEDS. The biblical number 40 of probation is well known; 41 signifies probation superseded (M. Mahan). Michael's 41 words comprise nine lines, the number for new beginnings which we met in the nine lines of all three Christmas Epistles. It is of course the present moment that counts in building that future. The namesake of January, Janus, the well-known god of initiation who looks both into the past and future, is called 'Master of threefold time' (R. Guénon 1995). The third, true face coming about between past and future, is invisible in its temporal manifestation. It is but an ungraspable instant. For this reason, Hebrew and Aramaic, for example, do not have a verbal form for the present. Realizing the present moment, or what we call presence of mind, is, however, vital! 'For as lightning that comes from the east is visible even in the west, so will be the coming of the Son of Man' (Mk. 13:27 and Lk. 14:24). Those who rise above the transitory, experience that the present contains all reality (cf. 'the Alpha and the Omega', which in the modern alphabet is A to Z; Rev. 1:8, 21:6, 22:13). 'Mercy is an attribute of power, not merely in sparing, but much more in uplifting, renewing, rehabilitating' (R.M. Benson). Mere succession is transmuted. Thereby, insistent spatial concepts are gradually raised into living, flowing form.

Twice in the yearly cycle a special opportunity for stimulating the consciousness arises at the crossing point when inner becomes outer (Easter) and outer becomes inner (Michaelmas). The liturgy places the word 'Now!' prominently at the end of the Inserted Prayers for these Festivals, and the Michaelmas Epistle, too. The word 'Now!' is thus heard once at Easter, and three times at Michaelmas during a single celebration. In the German, moreover, even the A to Z is heard three times, or actually twice three times (*'vom Anbeginn/ So jetzt und durch alle Zeitenkreise'*). Here and now the living light of heaven may shine; 'truths of the Real World in the language of this ... truths which are bright shafts of light breaking through into our darkness' (J.B. Phillips). Further lessons can be learnt from noticing the exact language for such concluding phrases of the Epistles, including the prepositions.

The 41 (= 21 + 20) lines of the Michaelmas Epistle consist of 196 = 98 + 98 words. Psalm 98, 'O sing to Yahweh a new song', tells how the whole universe is renewed by the Great King. Three times it speaks of salvation: 'All the ends of the earth have seen the salvation of our God' (v. 3). The gematria of the Hebrew for 'the salvation of our God' is 888, the special number of 'JESOUS' in Greek (ΙΗΣΟΥΣ). Jesus means 'saviour'; thus 'All the ends of the earth have seen Jesus.' We are told to burst into singing and music-making (vv. 4-6); even the sea, the rivers and the mountains join in to welcome the righteous Judge of the Earth (vv. 7-9).

'We stand with Him in the last days' (H. Scott Holland). Michael as ever stands before (not, for instance, 'beside' or 'instead of', but 'before') the Holy Trinity itself. The tenses of the verbs describing his deeds cover the past and the present and include a vista into the future—if we are willing. What are we to contribute? Through Michael's power we can be rid of earthly chains. The path of spiritualization that he demands is but another word for free cooperation. Towards this we have been led; towards this we have been yearning. Michael 'draws the free power' (the adjective 'free' is the 88th word of the Epistle). In our age, the Countenance of Michael as the third, 'middle' face can be glimpsed within. He assumes a particular gesture as he looks for spiritual deeds from spiritually free human beings. Michael inspires recognition of our latent divinity (Ps. 82:6, Jn. 10:34). In The Act of Consecration of Man itself, then, Michael himself has been our teacher all along, repeatedly pointing to 'Christ in you, the hope of glory' (Col. 1:27). Christ is creating the Heavenly Jerusalem already 'Now'. 'Now the dwelling of God is with men' (Rev. 21:3); 'your God will be your glory' (Isa. 60:19). Where is Michael, his captain, freshly inspiring human hearts and human utterance, speaking and singing on the Earth today in RENEWED 'songs of praise'?

'Is any one of you in trouble? He should pray. Is anyone happy? Let him sing songs of praise.' (James 5:13)

TRINITY

The Father-God be in us!
The Son-God create in us!
The Spirit-God enlighten us!

[Trinity Epistle]

Conscious of our humanity, we feel the divine Father.
He is in all that we are.
Our substance is His substance.
Our being is His being.
He moves in us through all existence.

Aware of the Christ in our humanity, we feel the divine Son.
He wields through the world as Spirit-Word.
He creates in all that we create.
Our existing is His creating.
Our life is His creating life.
He creates through us in all the soul's creating.

Grasping the Spirit through our humanity, we feel the healing
God.
May He shine through the world as Spirit-Light.
May He shine in all that we behold.
Our beholding be drenched with his Spirit-Light.
May He graciously receive our knowing into His life shining with
Spirit.
May He fill with Spirit all the ways of our human soul.

Trinitatis[11]

Der Vatergott sein in uns!
Der Sohnesgott schaffe in uns!

Der Geistgott erleuchte uns!

*In Bewusstsein unserer Menschheit erfühlen wir den göttlichen Vater.
Er ist in allem, was wir sind. Unsere Substanz ist seine Substanz. Unser
Sein ist sein Sein. Er geht in uns durch alles Dasein.*

*Im Erleben des Christus in unserer Menschheit erfühlen wir den gött-
lichen Sohn. Er waltet als das Geist-Wort durch die Welt. Er schafft in
allem, was wir schaffen. Unser Wesen ist sein Schaffen. Unser Leben ist
sein schaffendes Leben. Er schafft durch uns in allem seelischen Schaffen.*

*Im Ergreien des Geistes durch unsere Menschheit erfühlen wir den
eilenden Gott. Er leuchte als das Geist-Licht durch die Welt, Er leuchte
in allem, was wir schauen. Unser Schauen sei durchtränkt von seinem
Geist-Lichte. Unser Erkennen nehme er wohlgefällig in sein geistleuch-
tendes Leben auf. Er durchgeistige alles Walten unserer Menschenseele.*

The Holy Trinity

'Everyone moved by the spirit is a son of God.' (Rom. 8:14. NJB).

THE Trinity Epistle is heard four times in the year, after Epiphany, after Pentecost, after St John's Tide—the longest period—and after Michaelmas. The specific festivals of the year periodically retreat, revealing the eternal activity of the Godhead in relation to the deeper awareness of our humanity. The Trinity Epistle may be taken as the tenth Epistle that helps to interpret the other nine. These all contain the word 'heart' in a developing process; the Trinity Epistle can omit the word only because it is *all* heart.

It may seem astonishing that the doctrine of the Holy Trinity is not actually stated in the New Testament. The concept is to be found emerging, 'overheard' rather than 'heard'. In the most practical statement in the New Testament, Paul expresses the complete unity of the divine activity: *'Through* Christ we have our access *in* one Spirit *unto* the Father' (Eph. 2:18). The most ancient form of the doxology is 'Glory be to the Father, through the Son, in Holy Spirit'. The Trinity Epistle's three verses (a, b, c) each begin with the pronoun 'in'; this word occurs ten times (3 + 4 + 3). Verse (a) also contains the word 'is' three times; (b) contains the word *durch* ('through') twice; (c) *in* and *durch* three times each.

The distinction of Being in the Godhead expressed as the three Persons of the Holy Trinity, is the most philosophical attempt to conceive God as Personal. The phrase 'the personality of God' was unknown to Christian theology until about 200 years ago. Personality ('egohood') is the highest category we know. A social context is not simply implied; personality is social by definition. A 'me' requires a 'you'; 'I' requires a 'Thou'.

It is said that our knowledge of the Trinity is based on analogy with our own nature. Our body, soul and spirit is a living analogy of the living Trinity, belief in which 'is not a distant speculation; the Trinity is that blessed family into which we are adopted'

(Austin Farrer; cf. Rom. 8, Gal. 4). 'We are triune, not because our chief functions are three—thought, desire, and will—for there might conceivably be more, but because our personality consists of a subject, an object, and their relation. A person is a subject who can become an object to himself, and the relation of these two terms is necessarily a third term' (J.R. Illingworth). And still, we might add, the person is one being. This may help us to see how the triune God can still be One. With God everything that proceeds from Him is real, is personal—His thoughts, His desires, His actions. 'Let there be …' and it happens; 'This is my Body', and it is. But that manifestation, His eternally begotten Son, is also Himself (Heb. 1:3). The relationship of Love is complete and perfect. And that relationship is also Him. 'The act of divine life seems to be, as it were, a circulating act, which as originative is called the Father, as derivative is called the Son, and as in continuous procession is called the Holy Ghost' (R.M. Benson).

It may be difficult to formulate, but in our consciousness, our experience and in the laying-hold of our humanity, we can and indeed have to approach God. According to Thomas Aquinas, God is in all creation in three ways: (i) by *essence* that includes the whole of creation, (ii) by *power*, enjoyed by the rational soul in a state of grace, (iii) by *presence*, when God's grace is lovingly responded to in prayer. St John of the Cross expresses the thought similarly. It is not hard to perceive the activity once again of the one Triune God. 'One is the number for the unity of God; three is the number of divinity revealing Itself' (R. Steiner. 15 Sept. 1907. GA 101. Tr. A.S.).

The Father

In later Old Testament times, the fatherhood of God was beginning to be felt: 'O Lord, thou art our Father' (Isa. 64:8); 'I am a Father to Israel' (Jer. 31:9); 'If then I be a father …' (Mal. 1:6). For St Paul, whose writings are the earliest of the New Testament, earthly fatherhood derives from that of God: 'the Father, from whom every family, whether spiritual or natural, takes its name …' (Eph. 3:15). Jesus took the unprecedented step of addressing

God as 'my Father' (for example, Jn. 5:17; 8:19; 15:1, 8, 10, 23, 24, and so on). Through His coming all human beings can regard themselves as children of God. We are within His substance, His Being, living 'beneath His wings' (Ps. 17:8, Matt. 23:37 and Lk. 13:34) like chicks around their mother, asking to be kept as the apple (pupil) of His eye. If we conceive 'God' as some remote, unknowable being, we can be sure to have wandered into unreal abstraction.

'He goes before His creatures like a Father', says the Creed. YHWH ('He Who causes to be') whose name in Hebrew is so close to the verb 'to be', also means 'to breathe'. He is the ground of our being and consequently the ground of the world at the same time. Nature only appears to be 'out there'. Our make-up may dictate the appearance, which is also necessary for practical purposes, but our judgement certainly does not conclude that appearances are final. The kingdoms of Nature 'belong' to us, though they were shed long ago on the path of evolution. 'Creation,' claims Paul, 'is full of expectancy ... waiting for the sons of God to be made known' (Rom. 8:19. KV), that is, human beings who will release her enchanted spirit. This spiritual process has already begun, and is indeed included in every Act of Consecration of Man. The consecration of the human being brings the redemption of Nature with it. Learning to see with the light of the Spirit is to see beyond the appearances. Indeed, we pray to be 'drenched' with His personal Spirit-light. Is this too concrete for the transcendentalist? The paradox is well-known: God is transcendent to His creation because He is utterly independent of it, yet immanent because it is totally dependent on Him. God is *not* aloof from his creation. It covers Him like a garment. The Creator is to be found at the centre of the world, stretched out in the form of a cross, as Plato knew (*Timaeus* 35-37).

The Trinity Epistle is not a Creed, though the subject relates, and a comparison can be fruitful. 'Going before' is easily pictured by an agricultural community as the figure of a shepherd leading his flock. Perhaps one reason why Psalm 23 is the most loved may be because it is so concrete and personal. In its six verses, the first-person pronoun occurs seventeen times. One of Hermann Beckh's revealing translations begins: 'He who says "I" in me ...' The psalmist pictures Yahweh, the Saviour-God of the Old Testament, enthroned as the 'Shepherd of Israel' feeding his flock (Ps. 80:1). This God cares!

The Son

When Christ declares, 'I am the good, the beautiful Shepherd', another moment of self-realization flashes up that He is the man-ifestation in human terms of the Saviour-God. 'Jesus is Lord' is probably the first Christian creed (see M. Barker 1992). He comes as our passionate lover. Paul, by declaring that Christ 'fills all in all' (Eph. 1:23), means that 'in Christ the fullness of deity is perpetually resident' (F.F. Bruce) seeking and saving those who are lost.

The Son, the Word of God, His agent in Creation, cannot cease from creating. It is His nature. For Him to create is to reveal Himself. The dearest child of the Godhead is humankind. One fact may seem to be missing in the Trinity Epistle: the original plan went somewhat awry. When error was allowed to creep in, it was nevertheless taken up into God's plan and changed into an ultimately greater good. Jesus Christ is 'the Righteous One' (I Jn. 2:1). God's righteousness has been vindicated by the sacri-fice and the resurrection of Jesus, who shared our human life and bore our errors that we might be able to partake of His divine life. The cross of Calvary revealed the eternal Cross in our fallen world. Nothing of God's creation exists outside Him. The Media-tor is the divine human being, the God-man. What keeps Him at the centre of the world is indescribable Love. In the Trinity Epis-tle, the mission of error, guilt, sin and death are alluded to only in the adjective 'healing'—'the healing God'. All the other Epistles speak of the need for healing. The Trinity Epistle presents the life of the Godhead in direct relation to our human existence as spir-itual, creative beings. If our perceptions were pure, we would recognize Who it is Who 'creates in us' (interestingly, in the Bible the Hebrew verb for 'create' is almost only used of God), and Who is gradually creating a new humanity from within it.

The Spirit

Rather than use the term 'Holy Spirit', The Act of Consecration of Man speaks more of 'the healing Spirit'. This is certainly a tremendous help in recognizing what for many people appears to be the most elusive Person of the Trinity. Not only was the Son born on the Earth, the Spirit, too, was born, or made available, at Christ's sending at a particular time (Pentecost). Indeed, in German *der heilende Geist* contains the root *heil*, meaning 'salvation', also the meaning of the name 'Joshua'—the Hebrew form of 'Jesus'; in full 'Jehoshua'[12] came to mean 'Yahweh is salvation', or 'healing'. Though present from the beginning 'stirring the waters' (Gen. 1:2), He works now in, between and through human beings, ever seeking channels to help, heal and restore. The early Christians knew a shared life in the Spirit given at baptism (Acts 19:1-7). 'The fruit of the Spirit is love, joy, peace, patience, kindness, goodness, faithfulness, gentleness, self-control' (Gal. 5:22-24. NIV). Now, if 'God was in Christ reconciling the world to himself, not counting their trespasses against them' (2 Cor. 5:19), we appear to be less than grateful when we attribute our virtues to ourselves! The Spirit would appear to be far more widespread than we give Him credit. Is He not sent by the Father and the Son to be our very soul?

> *Low before Him with our praises we fall,*
> *Of Whom, and in Whom, and through Whom are all;*
> *Of Whom, the Father; and in Whom, the Son;*
> *Through Whom, the Spirit, with them ever One.*
>
> [Abelard, 12th century]

Conclusion

'Prayer is loving God in act so that the divine Love may communicate itself to us, and through us to the world.' (Thomas Aquinas)

SOME observations could be made on the place of the Epistles in the yearly cycle of The Act of Consecration of Man. A main polarity of the year (corresponding to summer / winter in the Northern Hemisphere) is shown by the Inserted Prayers for St John's Tide and Christmas, which are both spoken after the Offertory. This is the turning point at the heart of the musical structure of the ritual itself. The Inserted Prayer of St John's Tide is addressed to 'IOANES', Gk. form of 'John', that he behold the deed of blessing at the altar. He is described as the devoted Proclaimer surrounded by the sphere of the Father, one whose inspired word is archetypal. The Inserted Prayer of Christmas is addressed to the Father of all being and speaks of our joining the 'Song of Sacrifice' of all nine hierarchical ranks of the spiritual world, singing the praises of the Saviour-God. We hear in the one of the cosmic Word and a human being, and in the other of cosmic singing and the redeemed community of human beings.

The other two turning points in the ritual are so to speak at the lowest and highest points (easily seen on a lemniscate pattern; see p. 52). Two inserts are to be found: the first after the Proclamation of the Gospel and the second after the Consecration. These two inserts are (i) the words which correspond to the Creed, and (ii) the Lord's Prayer. These are both archetypal compositions and in themselves also present a polarity. The reworked Apostles' Creed is set in the form of twelve statements of verities that are worthy of meditation. The priest says these words as an individual human being with and for the sake of the assembled congregation, having temporarily disrobed both as celebrant (chasuble) and as priest (stole). The Lord's Prayer, the pattern for all prayer, can be experienced as forming the climax to each celebration. It is spoken in a consciousness of joining the whole world at prayer. Including the doxology and the 'Yea, so be it, Amen', its structure is ninefold (Adolf Saphir with the doxology; Jakob Boehme and Christoph Rau ninefold without the doxology). Incidentally, 'Amen' is one of God's names: *El-Amen*—'God [whose name is] Truth [in the sense of 'troth' or faithfulness]' (Isa. 65:16).

The nine seasons are completed by a tenth, Trinity. This season comes at the four 'in-between' times in the year. It can also interpret the whole yearly cycle. Not only do the seasons form triads (as noted above), but each triad can be regarded as relating to the Holy Trinity. This concept, like many others, need not be taken merely schematically, as a door to perception it can reveal further insights (see Appendix 2).

It is a fact that certain words are *not* used in the Epistles—for example, Jesus, faith, belief, sin, church, bread, wine—and certain theological concepts that we might expect are also missing. As noted above, this does not imply that these things are essentially absent. For example, 'Jesus' (Heb. 'Joshua'), meaning 'Saviour', may legitimately be included in all cognates of the word *Heil*, meaning 'salvation', from the heart that feels 'the Salvation in the womb of worlds' during Advent, to Salvation's announcer, IOANES (meaning 'Yahweh is gracious'), at St John's Tide; moreover *der heilende Gott*, 'the healing God', would be understood in New-Testament times as 'the spirit of Jesus'; the full name 'Jehoshua' means 'Yahweh is salvation'. Only God can save! Familiar older expressions have been re-expressed in the Epistles in an appropriately spiritually exact and devotionally adequate way. This claim is implied in the Epistles themselves—The Act of Consecration of Man originates from Christ (Pentecost Epistle). Behind human words and deeds are His words and deeds. The emphasis is on His life within humanity. That is, we hear His contemporary voice in liturgical words of renewal, of which Michael is the Guardian. Michael is the archangelic countenance assumed for our age by Christ, the God of human beings. The conclusion of the Michaelmas Inserted Prayer reveals his place as the mediator between the Trinity and the human heart. He stands, as it were, directly before God, in order to prepare us for the highest.

Rudolf Steiner

Marie Steiner

The existing liturgies of the Church, the New Testament, too, were all once written down by human hands. The part played by temple roots, oral tradition, extemporary prayer and so on, has retreated behind the text. How do we contemplate Rudolf Steiner as the inspired liturgist? A possible and worthwhile listing of his Christian virtues has not been undertaken here.[13] This all-round researcher is in a class of his own. Steiner (photo: left), our leading Church Father, is a modern prophet (cf. Amos 3:7, Eph. 4:11-13). He began his career as a scientist, also worked as an artist, finally dying in his studio in Dornach. He collaborated with other artists, including Edith Maryon, and especially with Marie Steiner-von Sivers (photo: above) in renewing the arts of the word, and in creating the new art of eurythmy, which is 'visible speech' and 'visible singing'—and which Michael Debus also calls 'visible karma', that is, 'visible deed' or 'action'. This comprehensive activity is Christian *because* it is completely human. We may regard Steiner as Michael's foremost follower, who would doubtless echo John the Divine, who called himself 'your brother and companion in the suffering and kingdom and patient endurance that are ours in Jesus' (Rev. 1:9). Apollos and Paul are 'only servants' (1 Cor. 3:5).

Richard Meux Benson

All Michael's followers will want to join in Michael's words: 'I am a servant just like you and all your brothers who are witnesses to Jesus. It is God that you must worship' (Rev. 19:10. NJB). No doubt Steiner hoped that worshippers of God learn to recognize Michael-inspired texts, for example, the Psalter, as suggested above (in the chapter on 'Michaelmas').

Dom Hubert van Zeller puts it in his usual succinctly profound way: 'Man does not create his prayers to God; he makes them up out of existing grace—out of the prayer of God. Man may think that his prayers come out of his head, but in fact they come out of the presence of God praying in his soul.'

Back in 1876, Richard Meux Benson (Founder and First Superior of the Society of St John the Evangelist, photo: above) eloquently expresses the basic facts of our lives in terms of glory, or revelation.

> It is not an earning of a future reward, but a revealing of a present strength. The appearing is not a coming to us, so much as a coming forth from within us, showing Himself truly within us, perfecting our faculties that we may apprehend that which is beyond our thought while we are here. The appearing is a revelation, so that when He shall be revealed, we also shall be revealed with Him in His glory, and He at His coming will be glorified in His saints and we in Him [cf. Col. 3:4 & 2 Thess. 1:10]. He will be glorified by the very fact of developing within us the power of beholding His glory. We shall be glorified in Him by the very fact, the very power, of seeing it. 'We shall be like Him, for we shall see Him as He is' [1 Jn. 3:2]. And all earthly life is only the training of the outer nature that we may become partakers of this heavenly vision, the bringing of our outer nature into subjection to Him, that there may be nothing in us of ourselves, but we may be the simple instruments of His manifestation of Himself, the elect mirrors of His glorious energy, the righteousness of God in union with Him [letter to Father O'Neill, 19 Oct. 1876].

Is not this passage directly relevant to our experience of The Act of Consecration of Man? 'Like the lamp, you must shed light among your fellows, so that, when they see the good you do, they may give praise to your Father in heaven' (Matt. 5:16 REB).

It may also be worthwhile just recalling that general consciousness has changed since the time of the formation of the traditional liturgies, as well as since the Reformation. The spotlight of the critical consciousness has increased. This is not all negative, for it has brought remarkable achievements. On the whole, critical scholarship is hailed as a positive development in so many fields. Much has been learnt, too, in the liturgical field. The point to be made here is that the critical movement also belongs to the Reappearance. Scholarship and technology, including the Internet, are but instruments, tools. The important question is whether human moral and spiritual development is progressing in tandem. Moral development demands human imagination, i.e. warmth of heart. Imagination is not unreal fantasy. Without it we cannot approach essential truth. An exact seeing of the heart is developed in the seasonal Epistles. 'Jesus says not "Why are you sinful?" but "Why are you afraid?"' (E.A. Abbott).

No one will deny that there are areas in religious practice still to be developed, in the fields of learning how to speak to enquirers, as well as to those antagonistic to Christian renewal. And there is a need for modern constructive theology, devotional literature, meeting youth, developing adequate music, and so on. Plenty of tasks for the here and now, not to mention the future! Perhaps attempts to appreciate the Epistles of The Act of Consecration of Man may help to stimulate the creative muse—for do they not call up a response in our lives?

'O God, my heart is ready, my heart is ready: I will sing and give praise with the best member that I have.' (Ps. 108:1. PBV)
'Pray as you can and not as you can't.' (Abbot John Chapman, writing to a nun)

Appendix 1
The Ethereal Realm of Concepts

'I AM: be not afraid.' (Matt. 14:27; Mark 6:50; John 6:20)

IN this section the aim is to get beyond possible specialisms and to suggest for the reader a *context* for the Epistles. I mention crucial themes and helpful researchers, and end with some thoughts on immediate developments and challenges. Living, creative thinking, according to Rudolf Steiner, is 'the only way forward'. But do we have to reinvent the wheel?

The main *literary form* to be found in the Epistles, mentioned though hardly followed up in these studies, is known as 'chiasm', or 'chiasmus', from the Greek letter *chi*: X. This mark is a universal and early symbol for the human being. It deserves a focus here. Most people have met chiasm in poetry and the various parallelisms of the Psalms and elsewhere in the Bible. Another name is 'correspondence'. Centuries passed before it was rediscovered. Chiasm is more than a technique,[14] where the first sentence / line has something to do with the last, the second with the penultimate, and so on, relating over a centre. Self-reference, become method, develops the forces of self-knowledge and resurrection in human thinking. These are archetypal musical forces (in an extended sense), where recollection and expectancy continually enhance awareness of the present. Music, for Goethe, an art involving 'the least material'; in Rudolf Steiner's formulation 'contains the laws of our ego' (29 Dec. 1915. GA 275). The 'laws' of the least material human principle involve relationships, movement—centre and periphery, concords and discords, reflection and metamorphosis.[15] Because these forces are primarily heard, the inner Voice is often termed *'musikē'* (understood by Plato as a mus-ish educational force) or 'melos' (inner tune, musical line), and is also known to poets (= both 'makers' and 'visionaries'). It is an audition antecedent to both our modern arts of music and poetry (Thasybulos Georgiades 1955).

The seer on Patmos hears 'a great Voice'.[16] 'I turned round to see the Voice that was speaking to me' (Rev. 1:12). Well, John sees a *Person*, and writes 'the revelation of Jesus Christ'. These very first words announce an account of the heavenly ascent of Jesus Himself (Barker 2000). In this section, stepping back from the Epistles that embody the inner Voice today, I assume an essay-style to write on *one* archetypal chiastic pattern. The chiastic pattern reveals the timeless and universal inner Voice linking to all the themes mentioned below: the primordial tradition, temple architecture and what went on within, the world's early prayers and lyrics, acknowledged outstanding artists of modern and more recent times… and the Epistles.

Firstly, some background context. René Guénon (1886-1951) on fundamental symbolism is still an exemplary teacher of 'the primordial tradition'. He draws on Eastern and Middle Eastern transcendental traditions in his aim to help in our plight facing the effects of Western materialism. More recently, Margaret Barker's work is among the most alive to Christian origins, including the Book of Revelation and the Christian liturgy. Single-handedly, this independent researcher has inaugurated 'temple theology'. With an impressive mastery of primary sources, above all she investigates the rich theme of initiation—'heavenly ascents'—and the rituals designed to heal the creation itself. Margaret Barker (photo: below) is at home in the cube-room, interpreting ancient texts with theologically disciplined imagination and scholarship, expressing her findings in an accessible style. Temple themes reappear, too, in Chartres Cathedral, another model of the universe,[17] the Globe Theatre, London, and other buildings.[18] Architecture, to Goethe 'frozen music', is similarly an educational force.

Margaret Barker

Secondly, the search for structural principles. Edward W. Bullinger (1837-1913), a leading Greek lexicographer and researcher of his day, edited and published a work by Thomas Boys, *A Key to the Psalms* (1890, 1899[2]) which reveals chiasm. In his introduction Bullinger summarizes this form, and again more fully under Boys's preferred term 'Correspondence' in *Figures of Speech used in the Bible* (363-93), and yet again in *How to Enjoy the Bible*. Throughout his astonishing *The Companion Bible*, this scholar marshals evidence of its universal presence. Another researcher, Sylvia Eckersley (2007), finds a chiastic pattern in the lineation of Shakespeare's plays as presented in *The First Folio* (1623), which she sees as an esoteric text. The pattern is traced for what it reveals rather than simply for information.

Milo Mahan

Another thread is the tradition of number in Scripture: Milo Mahan (1819-1870; photo left), together with Richard Meux Benson on the Psalter, are (I suggest) indispensable. These interpreters lead beyond mere statistical surveys. The technique of gematria, and so on, have been out of fashion at least since the Enlightenment. To interpret the phenomena, it would seem responsible to try to understand the modality. The main issue is to get beyond static labels by recognizing processes. Speaking to 'the workers' (skilled craftsmen!), Rudolf Steiner assigns the magic of number to the sixth grade of initiation, 'Sun Hero' (Dornach, 8 March 1924. GA 353). In addition to ancient Mystery traditions, the artistic examples of Bach and Shakespeare as revealed by recent research (see Bibliography) provide the present writer occasion for deep thought. The centre of drama was moving from the medieval altar to the stage, drawing room and eventually the theatre and concert hall. How did these artists (Bach and Shakespeare), who made a permanent impression at the beginning of our modern age, manage to reinvent a central Western esoteric-and-exoteric tradition and basically found our modern, democratized arts? Being born at the right time helped, but that important circumstance can't explain everything.

Thirdly, a further context for chiasm itself. Rudolf Steiner left important clues concerning chiasm, though without mentioning the term, especially in his remarks on good 'style' (*Speech and Drama*, 7 Sept. 1924. GA 282). Earlier, in the concluding lecture on John's Gospel (Hamburg, 31 May 1908. GA 103), surveying catharsis, meditation and the seven stages or grades of initiation, Steiner likens reading his beloved work of art [*sic*] *The Philosophy of Freedom* (1894. GA 4) to playing a composition on the piano— that is, playing a score on a keyboard built for the basic scale of 7 notes (+ 5 chromatic notes). He describes his book as a 'logically arranged organism'. Most readers fail to see beyond the logical arrangement, the intellectual dress, to the 'organism' itself. They fail to become proactive. Steiner's terms 'grades', 'keyboard', 'scale', 'organism' all point to the number seven, traditionally the number of *life*. Your reading has to be recreative, proactive, Steiner insists. Reading *through* the body of the text, that is, be aware of the *movement* between the lines and words (Dornach 22 & 25 Feb. 1924. GA 278: 72. 93f.), you glimpse the life, and it is at the same time your own. It helps, practically speaking, if you achieve the right tempo in reading. Steiner's analogy is a down-to-earth, nitty-gritty, musical technique. Technique = 'how it's done'; in *this* case the form reflects *and produces* the spiritual activity. *The Philosophy of Freedom: Some Results of Introspective Observation following the Methods of Natural Science* (the exact title, missing in *all* the files available online) presents a marriage of true mysticism and true science. The reader arriving at 'moral intuition' meets Meaning itself; we perceive the inner Voice and are aware of doing so. The method is based on a musical-liter-ary technique. Music is based on a pattern of 7 notes (the scale); the perfect, 'organic' literary unit is comprised of a pattern of 7 sentences. Moreover, 'Everywhere, in all realms of life, the number seven can be observed as a kind of number of perfection (*Vollkommenheitszahl*). There is no superstition or magic in this' (R. Steiner, 15 Sept. 1907. GA 101). But the music of humanity, already heard in history as the 'still, small Voice', and the iden-tity of the Psalmist's 'Chief Musician' (cf. Ps. 22:3), *is* in this!

Is the pattern an *impaled butterfly*? To say this is like saying the keyboard is not the music, that the angle-gestures of music eurythmy, and chiasm itself, are but 'systems'. Well, for exam-ple, sonnet-forms and sonata-form/s are also 'systems'—not moulds! In life, an ordering system—better 'form'—concerns the etheric level ('*Ätherreich der Begriffe*'—'the etheric realm of concepts'; Rudolf Steiner, *The Philosophy of Freedom*, Second Appendix, sentence 32, the fourth central sentence of the form [4 x 7] + 4 + [4 x 7]). We all know an ignorant application turns a matter into its opposite. The question, clearly, is *how* musicians overcome the keyboard, *how* eurythmists reveal melos, the melodic line, through showing the feelings in moving between what sounds, indeed, how artists compose in the first place—and how authors, especially poets and liturgists, avoiding didacticism, allow a chiasmic text to 'write itself' (if it may be expressed in that way). To ring true the text, including prose, is to sound inevitable, even spontaneous. The 'virtuoso' (Steiner's word) through discipline has overcome the technical challenges; these disappear from view, leaving the artistic experience to speak. We are interested to know and admire the techniques only in so far as they help us to appreciate even more that which we experience. The pianist and eurythmist don't despise their instruments; neither does the Christian despise the Cross. *'Impale'*? We didn't need to do the nailing on 3 April CDE 33, claims H. Scott Holland, nor do we need to continue to do so with His etheric, or subtle body, the living human blueprint manifesting today.

F.F. Bruce

'The *one valid proof* of divine inspiration is the "inward work of the Holy Spirit bearing witness by and with the word in our hearts"', F.F. Bruce reminds us (photo: left).[19] For this outstanding theologian—and speaking for most people—biblical numerics and gematria are suspect when brought as proof of divine inspiration. Clearly, sensationalism and mechanical 'proofs' are what is suspected.[20] Steiner certainly appeals to the witness of the heart, giving only broad clues about 'style' (GA 282, cited above). In this way he respects the freedom of his hearers. How else would they become responsible? At the very beginning of *The Philosophy of Freedom* (Second Appendix—actually the revised Foreword to the 1st edition, 1894; sentences 5 and 6), the philosophical basis of his life's work, he cites Schiller on the reflection of the heart.

Wahrheit suchen wir beide, du außen im Leben, ich innen
In dem Herzen, und so findet sie jeder gewiss.
Ist das Auge gesund, so begegnet es außen dem Schöpfer;
Ist es das Herz, dann gewiss spiegelt es innen die Welt

[F. Schiller, *aus Motivtafeln*]

Truth seek we both—Thou in the life without thee and around;
I in the heart within. By both can Truth alike be found.
The healthy eye can through the world the great Creator track;
The healthy heart is but the glass which gives Creation back.

[F. Schiller (from Votive Tablets, *tr. E. Bulwer Lytton*)]

[Prose tr.: Both of us seek for truth—in the world without you seek it, I in the heart within; both of us will doubtless succeed. If the eye be sound, it meets the Creator from without; if the heart be sound, then doubtless the world is mirrored within.]

In the second part of this Second Appendix, science and art are regarded as combined through the analogy of musical composition—'All true philosophers were *artists in the realm of concepts*' (sentence 47, emphases original). Composition, we know, is a precise art; every 'improvisation' is in fact always prepared; 'kissing the muse' is only part of it. Take the theme of the *Enigma Variations*, Elgar's 'dark saying'; was the composer celebrating *pi* (π)?[21] But beyond all speculation, recent detailed research (H. Kluge-Kahn, H. Thoene) into Bach's celebrations of divine creativity, or the Holy Spirit, demonstrates his application of traditional mysticism. Through the magic of number, Bach aimed to reflect the Creator Spirit, for Whose inspiration the Trinity Epistle also prays.

Steiner's lectures on number not only convey the traditional wisdom concerning their qualities, but at the same time point to general experience. He also advises eurythmists to play the seven-note scale (that is, not twelve abstract notes) and simply experience it—'The human being is a musical scale' (GA 278: 61, 65). It is not an impossible exercise. However that is, we *all* live the week—always the same, yet always different—a human rhythm that retains the names of the heavenly planetary deities. 'Be you therefore perfect, even as your heavenly Father is perfect' (Matt. 5:48), the Teacher of the Sermon on the Mount demands, linking to the heart of the Pentateuch (Lev. 19:2), reading 'perfect' for 'holy'. 'Getting it right' and 'making it your own, assimilate', summarizes the attempt to unite content and form, Heaven and Earth. This is the mature artistic ideal and, at the same time, the sacramental principle which, theologians tell us, 'continues the Incarnation'.

C.S. Lewis

A beginning can be made by getting the details in order, or rather by recognizing when they already *are* in order. Such is my real reason for attempting the present study. In case the subject still appears abstract—though we all live the concrete, weekly rhythm—let's briefly note just two major artistic achievements. C.S. Lewis's secret of over 50 years has now been revealed. For his seven, now world-famous, Narnia stories (1950-56), Lewis (photo: left) took inspiration from the seven planets of pre-Copernican cosmology, somewhat like Gustav Holst did for his orchestral suite *The Planets*, op. 32 (1914-1916), but in Lewis's case he kept it strictly secret. The astrological planets, Lewis wrote, are 'spiritual symbols of permanent value'.[22] With the further evidence of his adult 'space trilogy', it seems Lewis may not have been as dismissive of anthroposophy as his friend Owen Barfield claimed—but for Lewis spiritual knowledge had to be artistic. Holst's masterpiece, Lewis's creation of Narnia, Bach and Shakespeare, Steiner's philosophy, John's Gospel, the Psalter and indeed Scripture itself—are all known worldwide. In different ways, the authors *all* interpret 'what is'. The evidence seems indisputable.

The seven-sentence chiastic 'organic' unit establishes the creative method out of 'what is', that is, it couldn't turn out otherwise. To repeat, the method to research reality arises out of the reality we all experience. In the *Philosophy of Freedom*, the central image of 'the tree', the exact middle of Chapter 4, is more than a metaphor; Temple Theology would recognize 'the Lady' here—she goes by many names. In short, our knowledge and reality have to 'correspond', they are 'akin', the mind and reality 'correlate', they 'cohere', as, for example, the philosophers Wilfrid Richmond and William Temple both insist. Like the weekly rhythm, the chiasmic rhythm is evolutionary. Steiner writes a single sentence in this direction in one endnote to *Christianity as Mystical Fact* (GA 8. 1902 Germ ed.: 176. Tr. A.S.): 'About the significance of the number seven, one can enlighten oneself [*kann man sich aufklären*] out of my [publication] *Occult/Esoteric Science*' (GA 13. 1910). The number seven is made to carry the whole description of the world and its processes—nothing abstract here! The facts of evolution have to be correct, Steiner admits, but the 'essential point' of the accounts is the *inner movement*, the 'style' of writing. As in an awake-dream or meditation, the student experiences tensions, and relaxations 'which cannot be written down except in musical notation' (GA 278, 25 Feb. 1924: 94), which notation—specifying relationships and values—is eminently rhythmical and numerical.

Like the pattern throughout evolution itself, the sentences of the 7-sentence unit relate 1-7, 2-6, 3-5 around the central sentence 4, which contains the essential *Umstülpung*, or 'turning inside out'. This form, then, goes beyond illustrating, or portraying ideas. Whole chapters of Steiner's written work, that is, a specific number of organic units, relate around a centre consisting of a variable number of sentences (of course, in the German; translators very occasionally alter the original sentence arrangement). Now, other rhythms are also at work in the Seasonal Epistles, but the central crossing is always to be found. Here I take the one rhythm as exemplary, since it (there are no doubt others) is to be found throughout Rudolf Steiner's entire *written* work (as distinct from the lectures, although researchers have discovered specific rhythms and a central turning point). My discovery was first announced in 'What kind of Tree is *The Philosophy of Freedom*?' written to mark the centenary of the first edition of *The Philosophy of Freedom* (copies first appeared in November 1893). This article appeared in German.[23]

More recent attempts on the seven-sentence chiastic form in Steiner's *The Philosophy of Freedom* (in three parts) and two worked examples on his reports on the lecture-courses on eurythmy, appeared in the *Newsletter: Section for the Performing Arts*, Dornach (RB 44, 45, 46 and 55, 56 respectively).[24] Rudolf Steiner did not regard Section-work of the School of Spiritual Science as 'specialist'. He emphasized loyalty to the General Section, for which the word 'representative' is sometimes suggested as an alternative translation of *'allgemein'* (general). Perhaps there is sense in the suggestion mentally to rename it 'Theological Section'? This is more than a joke, since that discipline reflects what goes on in the General Section. Theology is essentially about 'I' and 'Thou' (vertical axis), and 'you' and 'me' (horizontal axis)—inner ascent for the sake of social development. 'Human Section'?—but, then, *all* the Sections centred in Dornach are human.

A way forward? Let us attempt to suggest a deeper picture of our situation. Recognition of musical form and of literary form is the very opposite of something dull. Bach, Bruckner, Debussy, Bartok, Hindemith, and Sofia Gubaidulina, we now know, are six composers who work with the rhythms of number. To their work, the work of Chopin can be added, at least on the evidence of the *24 Preludes for the Piano*, op. 28. If there is one supreme work for the piano (according to musicologist Henry Finck (1854-1926), echoed by Chopin scholar Jeremy Nicholas) it has to be this work. The reason, I submit, ultimately rests on the fact that in this work music itself wakes up to its own nature. The consciousness-soul, we are told, has to be consciously developed—we are beginning to appreciate the classical Chopin! This cycle—not a collection—is, firstly, a homage to Bach. It celebrates the tonal system itself as a spiritual journey. The methods of correspondence, revealed to a detailed investigation of the score, musically exploit the potentials of the numbers and relationships in the circle of fifths.[25] Debussy, one composer who opened the door to the twentieth century, was mentioned at the founding of The Christian Community for a direction to develop service music. Imitating sonorities is not meant, much more likely *the study of form*. Are amateur musicians at home with the phrase 'melody in the single note'? The phrase is most likely understood by priests in another terminology.[26] Well, it is central to the principles of chiastic form that most people *can* appreciate, for it demonstrates the very principle, firstly of generation and—when you get involved—of regeneration itself.

Menorah

The *Menorah*, the seven-branched, chiastic candlestick in the Temple (see Fig. left: c2 Menorah motif, Synagogue, Capernaum), represented the presence of the Lord; it is echoed on the altars of The Christian Community. Does perhaps 'the key of the house of David' (Isa. 22:22) point to it? If Rev. 3:7 'is claiming Jesus as the new high priest' (Barker 2000), then He commands the creative process that we already find in the creations of the divine musician David. He has not a song that does not pray, or a prayer that does not sing. The evidence suggests all the modern artists mentioned above are also aware of this process in their own creating. Steiner observes that the symbolism of Solomon's Temple made it 'the central star of the Earth' (Basel, 21 Dec. 1916. GA 173), no doubt central in space and time as well as on other levels. Its hymnbook was the Psalms of David; its priests are termed 'angels' in biblical and rabbinical texts. The latest research confirms the Temple tradition as the central Western esoteric-exoteric tradition. God entered the Temple when music sounded (2 Chron. 5:13). Bach wrote in his Calov-Bible: '*NB. With a devotional music God in His glory is present at all times*' (Kluge-Kahn. 1985: 26). We should recall that Bach sat at the feet of the mystics. The theologian J.E.L. Oulton[27]—i.e. not a professional musician—mentioning the Passion music, declared Bach 'is not unworthy to be named in the same breath as St Paul'.

Now, it is interesting to note one detail about the art of eurythmy. Steiner declares that performers of eurythmy may stimulate a question in the hearts of the viewers, 'Well, are all these people angels?' (Stuttgart, 30 April 1924. GA 277a: 142). The context shows this is not a decorative remark. Moreover, the first actual *word* to be carried out in eurythmy (along with I-A-O, one of the names for God) was the word 'Hallelujah' (22 Sept. 1912. GA 277a: 41), which appears in 15 psalms of the 150 comprising the Psalter. Are, then, the activities of the staff in the Temple reborn in the arts of the Goetheanum-impulse? Practitioners of the 'visible word' (R. Steiner, *Nachrichtenblatt*, 2 March 1924) today, including performing artists and Christian priests, share the task of renewal. 'It is when the word is added to the element that the sacrament results as if [it is] itself also a kind of visible word', Augustine explains (*On the Gospel of John*, Trac. 80.3). Today's 'staff' of a worldwide movement surely include musicians and priests of The Christian Community. Certainly, professional music conferences take place, in particular on the continent.

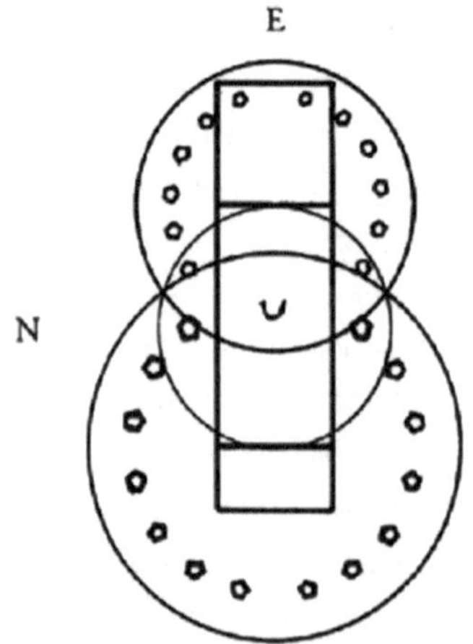

Plan of the First Goetheanum and of Solomon's Temple (superimposed)

To come up to date, Michael Debus is widely appreciated for his insights into eurythmy as 'visible karma'—'karma' is the concept of 'deed', or 'action'—at a recent professional eurythmy conference in Dornach. In a word, we live in a 'sacramental universe', to use William Temple's phrase. 'Visible Word'; spoken Word; presence of the Lord; the evolutionary, creative sevenfold path …—what further collaboration could develop from this? Now that Dr Debus[28] has pointed out the ancient Atlantean roots of the new performing art of movement with special reference to the T-I-A-O-A-I-T reflecting eurythmy-form, perhaps a discussion of reflective artistic method may continue the exchange? We don't need to get lost in Chinese history, but we do need to know the past in order to make meaningful steps forwards with our contemporaries.

The chiasmic form is a Tree of Life. The Tree of Life is human, singing unceasingly at the centre of the world. We need not baulk at attempting a comprehensive view. A comprehensive view would perforce acknowledge bona-fide research wherever it appears. The growing point appears where it will. The divine self-revelation, *ehye asher ehye* (Ex. 3:14), conventionally translated 'I AM WHO / THAT I AM', or 'BEING IS BEING', but better, the One 'WHO CAUSED TO BE, AND CAUSES TO BE, AND WILL CAUSE TO BE' (Targums to Exodus 3), is elucidated by Martin Buber:[29]

> The first *ehye* simply gives the assurance: I shall be there (ever and ever with My host, with My people, with you)—thus you do not need to conjure me. And the following *asher ehye*, according to all the parallels, can only mean: as I Who will always be there, as I ever and ever will be there, that is, as I ever and ever will want to appear. I Myself do not anticipate My forms of appearance; and here you think to be able to conjure Me with some means, to appear here and not elsewhere, now and not some other time, thus and not otherwise!

The struggle today with what threatens, including fashions, prejudices and worse, distracts us from ourselves. For those who still feel protective, allow me to state my position: musicians serve from the first note to the last. Music exists not for musicians, but for those who can listen. Christianity, too, proclaims the Good News for those who can listen. Faith, says Paul, comes from hearing (Rom. 10:17); eurythmy, too, comes from proactive listening (25 Aug. 1919. GA 294). 'Ears Thou hast dug for me' (Ps. 40:6 Heb.), that is, a nature 'formed for obedience' (Benson 1901, I. 23. Kay 131; Christianus I, 237f). Speaking for myself, I would keep abreast of the times, believing only my best will do in all endeavours to distribute some crumbs for a starving world and, yes, in the face of widespread dissemination of information on the Internet. Like the printing press, the Internet is but a tool; its influence can already begin to be evaluated. As regards spiritual work, an intensification is certainly demanded, something (as ever) inevitably uncomfortable.

A few further words may be allowed. Although I do respect writers who cite one sole, pre-eminent author, I see my own task everywhere as that of a catalyst. It annoys many people; they can't pigeonhole me and my faults are too obvious. As a teacher, too, I may not cease from my own research while at the same time aiming ultimately to become redundant. This policy, I submit, neither dilutes nor intellectualizes anything. God is not mocked. Furthermore, as René Guénon points out, the formal distinction between sacred and secular isn't strictly valid. Life is a whole; at most, he admits, some people might entertain 'a secular point of view'. Where can spiritual seekers find further suggestions? In the study-material to the English translations of Rudolf Steiner's lecture-courses *Eurythmy as Visible Singing* (GA 278) and *Eurythmy as Visible Speech* (GA 279), together with the accounts of the early indications (GA 277a), the spiritual sources of this new art are discussed. The former work (GA 278) now in its fifth edition (RSP) includes a composer's manifesto that influenced Steiner, J.M. Hauer, *Interpreting Melos*—Steiner not only kept abreast of the latest developments but did his utmost to show the way forward by his own example. In this lecture-course (GA 278) of eight lectures, for example, every single numerical reference is significant.

Hermann Beckh

Translations of valuable earlier studies are appearing in print; for example, Friedrich Rittelmeyer *The Holy Year* (Floris 2019) and *Letters on John's Gospel* (TL 2022). The four chapters of *Christus*, Rittelmeyer's final masterpiece (tr. 'Christ' in MS), unfold like the four great parts of The Act of Consecration of Man itself. Rittelmeyer (1872-1938), an extraordinary man of prayer, as Emil Bock emphasizes (included in F.R. *Letters on John's Gospel*, TL 2022, 303-307), leads the reader into higher realms of listening. An article on Rittelmeyer and music appeared in *The Threshing Floor* (May/June 1988: 15-18), and also in *Die Christengemeinschaft* (60. Jg. 3. März 1988: 142-45). However, to crown all reassessment, the *Collected Works* of Hermann Beckh (1875-1937, photo: p.124) in 16 vols. are in English translation. The claim can now be made against all counter-suggestions: Hermann Beckh, universal scholar, could be a mighty guiding star for the 21st century.

In conclusion, let's now attempt to gaze briefly at the Sun. We read in *The Wisdom of Solomon* that God has 'set all things in order by measure and number and weight' (Wisdom 11:20). If mathematics and music cohabitate the Inspirational realm, awareness of the dangers *prepares* the Michaelic explorers; it should not hinder their starting-out. Is there an issue of distinguishing between cosmic intelligence and its mere earthly shadow? Arithmetic—not quite the activity we met at school—began metaphorically with Abraham, as did the Church itself with the Call of Abram (Gen. 12:1ff). These are *both* reflective activities. Study of a text by Shakespeare, or a score by Bach, Chopin or Debussy, *increases* appreciation and the ability to interpret them. Moreover, we are to read the accounts of spiritual science, including its philosophical basis, 'like musical scores'—assimilate and *play* them, just as we did in learning our mother tongue. And to play the piano; in fact, we assimilate to learn almost *any*thing![30] Meditations on the central sacrament of the seven, where 'measure and number and weight' are present as rhythm, proportion, and form, can be helpful precisely in getting beyond fear of an 'earthly shadow'. The God of human beings Himself—in the Bible, the word for 'create' is nearly always used of God—is the initiating Creator in everything human. He looks out of the pages, for instance, of *The Philosophy of Freedom,* though people repeatedly assume it must be His opposite—it is rather their own disbelief they see. He is finally mentioned towards the end, around the Golden Section of Chapter 15 (sentences 62-3 of 101; rings a bell?), after the 2 x 7 chapters. The journey is from periphery (*Zipfel*—'coat-tail') to centre. Of course, in the Apocalypse the concrete explanation is familiar that 'the seven stars are the angels of the seven churches, and the seven lamps are the seven churches themselves' (Rev. 1:20). It is further revealed Who is 'in the midst of heaven' ('in the midst', not 'before' the throne, as in some translations), with His seven horns and seven eyes, 'which are the seven spirits of God sent forth *into all the earth*' (Rev. 5:6).

Incidentally, the vision of the heavenly throne (the cube-room *was* heaven) in Revelation 4 was the only part of the New Testament that Alfred Heidenreich felt he could 'with complete honesty' proclaim from the altar during the very first weeks of his distinguished career, before he brought The Christian Community to the British Isles.[31] Through the language of vision, he came quite soon to realize Who is 'speaking-singing, singing-speaking' out of the page. The biblical 'new song' is better translated 'renewing song' (e.g. Ps. 96; Isa. 42:10, Rev. 5:9-10). In this light, I submit, research of text and score can safely enter into the details (Matt. 5:16).

Rudolf Steiner

It is not unusual for a member of The Christian Community to know the Epistles by heart. I have simply used GA 345 to check the lineation. Computations in my text always refer to the German text. My part in producing this booklet, as already stated, is hardly more than that of a catalyst. It may also be noted—in case of any doubt—that my respect for the renewed sacraments precludes any association with individuals wishing to start up religious movements of their own (although I haven't met any). I rather take the lesson as applying to ourselves. The Church, it is promised in the New Testament, will withstand 'the gates of Hades' (Matt. 16:18). On the other hand, without Imagination and even Inspiration, warned Rev. Ormond Edwards (Matlock Conference, c.1984), 'the Spirit will go elsewhere'. Renewal by definition does not mark time; it promotes life. Welcome, twenty-first century! Welcome, our approaching centenary! 'Amen. Come Lord Jesus,' declares the Seer, concluding the New Testament itself. Faith in the continuing revelation of the Word is my only justification for this very small contribution attempting to hear 'what the Spirit is saying to the Churches'—A.S., 1999, rev. 2013, 2023.

When studying, for example, a very difficult book, it depends less on comprehending the content, more on entering the author's line of thought and to learn to think with him. Hence the pupil should find no book too difficult; if he does, it means only that he is too easy-going to think. The best books are those we have to take up again and again, books we cannot understand immediately but have to study sentence by sentence. [The stage of study] depends not so much on what we study as how we study. If we study great truths, for instance the planetary laws, we develop important lines of thought, and this is what really matters. If we say that we want more moral teaching and nothing about planetary systems, we show great egoism. True wisdom engenders a moral life.

[Rudolf Steiner. *At the Gates of Spiritual Science*. GA 95. Stuttgart, 4 Sept. 1906. Tr. A.S.; Germ. ed.: 140f.]

Raphael (1483-1520): Ezekiel's Vision (c. 1518). Palatine Gallery of Palazzo Pitti, Florence, Italy

Appendix 2
Computations

(Computations refer to the German text.)

FESTIVAL	LINES	WORDS
	Epistle / Insert	Epistle / Insert
Advent	44	170 (92+78)
	16	47
Christmas	9, 9, 9 + 6	30, 36, 33 + 24
	12	79 (39+40)
Epiphany	27 (11+4+11)	74
	11	24
	(*Trinity* i)	
Passion Tide	13, 13	41, 36
	13	34
Easter	13, 13	36, 24 + 13
	36 (20 [=11+9]+6+10)	101
Ascension Tide	20 (7+6+7)	68 (34+34)
	17 (10+7 or 5+5)	46 (23+23)
Pentecost	20 (7+7+6)	58
	17	53
	(*Trinity* ii)	
St John's Tide	43 (6+8+4+7+10+8)	141
	13	33
	(*Trinity* iii)	
Michaelmas	41 (13+14+14)—4 sentences:	
	(13+11+8+9)	
	196 (98+98)	
	15 (2 sentences: 9+6)	75
	[Michael's direct speech:	
	9	41]
Trinity (iv)	17 (3 sections 5+6+6)	129 (33+46+50)
TOTAL:	447 lines	1601 words

[NB central lines and central words]
A few examples of gematria, etc.:
13—rebellion *and* redemption
15—Jah
17—number of God's covenanted people (e.g. 9 x 17 = 153
     fishes)
41—= 40 (biblical number of probation) superseded. [J.S. Bach =
        41, Bach = 14, David, in
           Heb. *dvd* = 14]
101—Michael, Jah Elohim, Malachi
888—Jesus (in Greek ΙΗΣΟΥΣ)

	FATHER	SON	SPIRIT
FATHER	Advent	Passion Tide	Pentecost
SON	Christmas	Easter	St John's Tide
SPIRIT	Epiphany	Ascension Tide	Michaelmas

(Fig. a) Trinity helps to explain the other seasons.

'become' it speaks	my self	World Physician
future-word	house of Earth	word of praise
		word of offering

has appeared	the self … shines	His word of flame …
song of sacrifice	your word go forth	in light's fullness of love
	… now and beyond	

life in Christ	… transfiguring earthly	A.C.M. … in our hearts
spirit-beam	with heavenly being	Follow me! …
of the star		heavenly light …
	song of praise	now and in all
		cycles of time

[Cosmic WORD becomes human DEED]

(Fig. b) A survey of some important words using the above scheme

Our heart can sense	the place of your heart	flames … from human hearts …
the salvation	is empty / burning	word of praise … souls

130

	sting of evil in the heart	keep themselves whole
prayer in our hearts the heart within us …	the heart is full … rejoicing healing power my heart praises	the word of flame … burn in our hearts …
to add warmth of heart …	we behold with	the visionary solemnity, that … prepares
radiant with heart's love	power in our souls … our hearts praise and HIM magnify	the heart of man for the light … Christ sends His power bearing spirit into human hearts … if Human beings feel the fire of their Hearts rightly enkindled

(Fig. c) References to the heart, arranged on the above scheme

Notes

1 'Any growth in the adaptation of the Liturgy to the uses for which it is designed—for bringing man's mind into larger contact with truth, man's soul into deeper love for the Saviour, man's will into more complete submission to the will of God—that is liturgical growth, and nothing else is' (Phillips Brooks. Address. 27, Oct. 1881. *Essays & Addresses*. New York: Dutton 1894: 97f.). This writer is famous for writing the hymn, 'O little town of Bethlehem'.

2 'Heavens' or 'sky'?—'*Himmel*' can mean both. Metaphors are two-edged and thereby create meaning (in science, too: Isaac Newton's apple is a metaphor for the Moon). Like the 'still small voice', literally 'voice of thin silence' (I Kings 19:12), the ambiguity—whisper or breeze?—is to be retained in translation (Prickett 1986). The expression 'the Heavens' (earlier translation) embraces the Earth and includes the inner imagery; does the 'sky' (rev. tr.) do this more adequately since the temple is all around us today, or does 'sky' tend to reduce, even fix the meaning? (Cf. 2 Cor. 12:2, Rev. 4:3).

3 Of Holland's sermon, Michael Ramsey (*From Gore to Temple*, 1960/ 2009: 45) wrote: 'I needs must think that this sermon is among the greatest of all time.' Holland's was the strong prophetic voice who, with the publication of *Lux Mundi*, ed. Charles Gore (1889), heralded a new Michaelic influence in the social and religious life in Britain before the Great War. The four addresses on sacrifice in *Logic and Life* were also pub. with an Easter address as *The Sacrifice of the Cross* (London 1879). In that year, too, there appeared George Bowen, *The Amens of Christ* and Phillips Brooks held his Bohlan Lectures on *The Influence of Jesus* that met the doubt, weakness and scepticism of the times (summarized & reviewed in Alexander V.G. Allen, *Life and Letters of Phillips Brooks*, Vol. 2. New York: Dutton 1901); finally, the 1879 lectures of Andrew Jukes, *The New Man*, London 1884, / Kessinger 2009/10, etc., an in-depth study of the 12 reiterated Johannine 'Amen'-sayings.

4 'The only Baroque thing about Bach,' claims the musicologist William Mann, 'was his wig.' Like Shakespeare, he too was 'not of an age but for all time' (Ben Johnson). Like a tremendous medieval cathedral, Bach's music portrays the unity of the starry, or astral, body—'the musician in us' (R. Steiner, Stuttgart, 10 April 1924 a.m. GA 308), whose 'basic force' is FAITH (R. Steiner, lecture Nuremberg,

2 Dec. 1911, in *The Golden Blade*, London 1964: 1-26 (online: https://
waldorflibrary.org/journals/164-golden-blade). More than any other composer, Bach established tonality, exploring the complete circle
of fifths. Moreover, through 'the magic of number', Bach shows his
profound studies in self-realization in the late instrumental cycles. It
is becoming increasingly clear this became artistically and thus so-
cially productive by marrying his total compositional technique to a
traditional number-code, including gematria, in order to cooperate
with the Creator's methods. According to the latest research (Kluge-
Kahn, H. Thoene), Bach's chosen models that conceal-reveal spiritual wholeness are the divine-human alphabet, the Christian Year, the
Heilsgeschichte (story of salvation), the Rosicrucian verse and much
more.

5 'Christianus' (II, 81), in his brilliant verse-by-verse, devotional, extended paraphrase of the whole Psalter as the prayer-book of Messiah, writes on Ps. 88:6: *'Thou hast set me in the lowest pit.* Thou hast
made Me to feel the condition of the sinner under the hiding of Thy
countenance, the horror of thick darkness, and the deeps of woe, in
order that I might deliver the penitent of destruction.'

6 'He did not purify our human nature in order that He might assume
it when purified. He purifies our nature by the act of assuming it'
(R.M. Benson. 1901. I. 39).

7 On the 153 fishes, see M. Mahan (1875), J. Michell (1972), David Fideler (1993) and Chr. Rau (2023). Painting on p. 74 of the miraculous
draught of fishes, by Duccio di Buoninsegna, 14th century.

8 Alexander Whyte, *Bible Characters from the Old and New Testaments*,
Grand Rapids. Kregel 1990. 707f.

9 R. Benaiah [attrib.]. *j. Ta'anit* 4.2. Margaret Barker. *The Great High
Priest*. London, New York: T&T Clark 2003. 117, 141.

10 John Eaton. *The Psalms*. London, New York: T&T Clark 2003. 13.

11 The facsimile of the Trinity Epistle is arranged in three block para-
graphs, as reproduced here in letterpress—*A.S.*

12 The Hebrew form of 'Jesus'; the dictionaries say Yasha, the Heb. root
of Joshua / Jesus had the dominant meaning 'to release a slave or
captive, often by ransom performed by a kinsman.'

13 See Hermann Beckh, 'The text of The Act of Consecration of Man and
the Old Latin Mass', in Rudolf Frieling, *Living Renewal*, TL 2024.

14 James L. Bailey & Lyle D. Vander Broek. *Literary Forms in the New Testament*. Louisville, Kentucky: Westminster/John Know Press 1992/
London: SPCK 1992. Chiasm is acknowledged throughout the Bible,
and in particular: 'A familiarity with chiasms is essential in the exe-

gesis of Paul and the larger Pauline tradition' (50). Recent works are citied, but no mention of Boys or Bullinger.

15 Though the stages of metamorphosis (Gk. μεταμόρφωση) cannot be logically deduced from what has gone before, the transitions can be revealed through a 'musical' meditation. The word 'metamorphosis', rather than the Latin 'transformation', is used in a neglected work in the tradition of Origen, Edward Meyrick Goulburn's Bampton Lectures, *The Resurrection of the Body* (Oxford 1850: 174, 181, 189, 199); likewise, the word 'interpenetration' (183, 186, 240), coined by Coleridge. The imagination alone can picture it, and indeed the law of polarity, the principle of life itself.

16 Sometimes rendered 'loud voice'. Gk. φωνην μεγαλην, 'great voice', also AV; Torrey (Aramaic reconstruction) 'great'; musicians say *forte*, 'strong'—power, not noise.

17 See, Donald Strachan, Chartres: *Sacred Geometry, Sacred Space*. Edinburgh: Floris Books. 2003; also 'Chartres Cathedral—A Sacred Geometry' (documentary with Keith Critchlow).

18 Joy Hancox, *The Byrom Collection*. London: Jonathan Cape. 1997.

19 F.F. Bruce, 'The End of the Second Gospel', *The Evangelical Quarterly* 17 (1945): 169-181.

20 'Numbers, in fact, symbolize principles rather than dogmas; they are suggestive rather than definitive; colourless in themselves, they readily assume the colour of surrounding objects; having, as it were, a negative and positive pole, their meaning takes a negative or positive hue according to the pole which happens to be presented' (Milo Mahan, 'Mystic Numbers' in *Collective Works*, II, 218).

21 http://en.wikipedia.org/wiki/Enigma_Variations

22 Quoted in Michael Ward. *Planet Narnia*. Oxford: OUP 2008: 43; see also M. Ward. *The Narnia Code*. Paternoster 2010; also as DVD 2011.

23 *Jahrbuch für anthroposophische Kritik* 1994. Lorenzo Ravagli (Hg.). Trithemius Verlag München: 83-98. (http://www.anthroweb.info/trithemius_verlag.html#.UhMoOxabKfQ)

24 Electronic files in both English and German can be downloaded from the Goetheanum website http://www.goetheanum.org/Newsletter.957.0.html?&L=1. The latest summary appears in Hermann Beckh, *Celebration*, TL forthcoming 2025.

25 Alan Stott, 'Chopin's Homage to Bach', Parts 1 & 2. *Newsletter: Section for the Performing Arts*, RB 38, Easter 2003 and RB 39, Michaelmas 2003 (Dornach), traces the emerging use of B-A-C-H (= B♭, A, C, B), the composer's use of number and his relationship to the traditional mystic path; analogues are suggested to the 12 'Verily, verily' sayings

of John's Gospel. Robert Kolben's exemplary analysis and critical comments, with answer from A.S., *Newsletter* RB 40, Easter 2004. See also, 'Robert Kolben (1929-2005)', *Newsletter* RB 43, Michaelmas 2005. The latest attempts regarding Chopin, Bach and Steiner appear in two contributions in the final volume of Hermann Beckh's Collected Works: *Hermann Beckh: A Celebration*, TL forthcoming 2025.

26 See Rudolf Steiner, *Eurythmy as Visible Singing* (GA 278), study-edition RSP 2019, Endnote 22, and p. 472f. The later page ref. is to Appendix 9 'Art as a Way—the Way as Art', 469-87, also in German as 'Kunst als ein Weg—Der Weg als Kunst' in the collection of studies *Der Toneurythmiekurs von Rudolf Steiner*, Stefan Hassler (Hg.), Dornach 2013, 40-55.

27 J.E.L. Oulton, *The Mystery of the Cross*. London: SCM 1957: 40.

28 Michael Debus, *Das Wesen der Eurythmie: Vergangenheitswurzeln und Zukunftswirklichkeit*. CH-Dornach: Verlag am Goetheanum. 2012.

29 Martin Buber. *Kingship of God*. London: Geo. Allen & Unwin. 1967: 106. German original: *Königtum Gottes*. Heidelberg: Verlag Lambert Schneider 1956[3]: 69. Buber translates Ex. 3:14: 'Ich werde dasein, als der ich dasein werde … So sollst du zu den Söhnen Jifsraels sprechen: ICH BIN DA schickt mich zu euch' (*Die Fünf Bücher der Weisung*. Berlin: Lambert Schneider 1950[3]/1976: 177).

30 Stephen Prickett, *Origins of Narrative: The Romantic Appropriation of the Bible*. Cambridge: CUP 1996.

31 Alfred Heidenreich, *Growing Point*. London: The Christian Community Press.1965: 79.

32 'I want an intelligent, well-instructed laity … I wish you to enlarge your knowledge, to cultivate your reason to get an insight into the relation of truth to truth, to learn to view things as they are, to understand how faith and reason stand to each other, what are the bases and principles of Catholicism.'
J.H. Newman, *Lectures on the Present Position of Catholics in England*. Lectures, Birmingham 1852. London: Burns, Oates & Co 1885 / London: Longmans, Green 1896: Lecture 9: 390; http://www.newman-reader.org/works/england/lecture9.html#strengthingod/
The word 'catholic' means 'universal'; we might accurately substitute 'non-sectarian Christianity'. Newman was close to being accused of heresy by claiming: 'In all times the laity have been the measure of the Catholic spirit'. He was canonized in 2019.

33 2 Cor. 3:1-3. Peterson. *The Message*. Colorado Springs: Navpress 2003.

Select Bibliography

For earlier titles, try *www.archive.org*; secondhand market (also Kindle eds.): www.*bookfinder.com/ abebooks.co.uk/ abebooks.com/ & amazon.co.uk/* Although I did not use the site, 1700 books are available at *http://www. sacred-texts.com* (NB reprint editions are constantly appearing for certain earlier publications.)

K.F. Althoff, *Das Vater Unser*. Stuttgart: Urachhaus 1978.

Margaret Barker,

—, *The Gate of Heaven*. London: SPCK 1991.

—, *The Great Angel: A Study of Israel's Second God*. London: SPCK 1992.

—, *The Risen Lord*. Edinburgh: T&T Clark 1996.

—, 'Atonement. The Rite of Healing', in *Scottish Journal of Theology* 49.1 (1996), pp. 1-20 (www.margaretbarker.com).

—, *The Revelation of Jesus Christ*. Edinburgh: T&T Clark 2000.

—, *The Great High Priest: The Temple Roots of Christian Liturgy*, London/ New York: T&T Clark 2003.

Owen Barfield, *Romanticism Comes of Age*. Sophia Perennis 2006/ Barfield Press UK 2012.

Hermann Beckh, *The Essence of Tonality* with *The Parsifal Christ-Experience*, etc. Tr. A.S and Anneruth Strauss. TL 2022.

Richard Meux Benson,

—, *The War-Songs of the Prince of Peace*, 2 vols. London: John Murray 1901; Isha Books 2013, ISBN 9789333184236 and ISBN 9789333184243 (online: www.archive.org), in a class of its own.

—, *Spiritual Letters of Richard Meux Benson*, ed. W.H. Longridge. London/ Oxford; Milwaukee 1924; Kessinger 2010, & online.

Kalmia Bittleston, 'The Three Crosses in Space', *The Christian Community Journal* 1954, 75-77 (photocopies: The Archivist, The CC, Hartfield Rd, UK-Forest Row, RH18 5DZ).

John Henry Blunt, *The Annotated Book of Common Prayer*. London, Oxford, Cambridge 1871[4], Ulan Press 2012 (contains a short commentary on the Psalter).

Emil Bock, *The Apocalypse of St John*. Edinburgh: Floris Books 2005[3].

Thomas Boys, ed. E.W. Bullinger, *A Key to the Psalms*. London & New York 1899², General Books 2012, Ulan Press 2012.

F.F. Bruce,

—, *The Epistle to the Ephesians*. London & Glasgow: Pickering & Inglis, 1961; Fleming H. Revell 1976; Marshall Pickering 1978.

—, *The Letters of St Paul*, Grand Rapids: Eerdmans 1965.

Martin Buber, *I and Thou*. Tr. R.G. Smith. Edinburgh: T&T Clark 1959, Important Books 2013, etc. The recommended translation.

Edward W. Bullinger: some titles are perhaps still available on www.archive.org

—, *The Witness of the Stars*. Grand Rapids, Mi.: Kregel 2003.

—, *Number in Scripture*. Grand Rapids, Mi.: Kregel 2006.

—, *Figures of Speech used in the Bible*. Grand Rapids, Mi.: Baker Book House 2011.

—, *How to Enjoy the Bible*. Grand Rapids: Kregel 2004.

—, *The Companion Bible*. Oxford 1909-21; Grand Rapids: Kregel 2012.

J.H. Charlesworth, ed., *The Odes of Solomon*. OUP 1973/ Cascade Books 2009.

Christianus, *The Christ of the Psalms*. 2 vols. London: Bickers 1872; Isha Books, 2013 (ISBN 9789333188111 and ISBN 9789333187381). (Also held in UK, e.g. by www.evangelical-library.org.uk).

Michael Debus. *Das Wesen der Eurythmie: Vergangenheitswurzeln und Zukunftswirklichkeit*. CH-Dornach: Verlag am Goetheanum 2012.

James Denney, *The Death of Christ*. London 1911; Forgotten Books 2012.

Austin Farrer, *The Crown of the Year*. Westminster: Dacre Press 1952.

Evelyn Francis, 'The Sign of the Cross', *The Christian Community Journal* 1948: 37-39 (copies from the Archivist, The CC, Hartfield Rd, UK-Forest Row, RH18 5DZ).

David Fideler, *Jesus Christ, Sun of God*. Wheaton Ill., Madras, London: Quest Books 1993.

Rudolf Frieling, *Hidden Treasure in the Psalms*. Edinburgh: Floris Books 1967.

Thrasybulos Georgiades,

—, *Music and Language*. CUP 1982/ *Musik und Sprache*. Wissenschaftl. Buchgesell. (wbg academic) 2018.

—, *Greek Music, Verse and Dance.* New York: Merlin Press 1955/ Da Capo Press 1973/ Germ. Ed. rev. & augmented: *Musik und Rhythmus bei den Griechen.* Hamburg: Rowohlt 1958.

René Guénon,

—, *The Symbolism of the Cross.* Sophia Perennis 2002/ *Die Symbolik des Kreuzes.* Aurum Verlag: Freiburg im Breisgau 2002.

—, *The Great Triad.* Cambridge: Quinta Essentia 1991.

—, *Fundamental Symbols.* Cambridge: Quinta Essentia 1995.

F.C.N. Hicks, *The Fullness of Sacrifice.* London: SPCK 1946/53.

Henry Scott Holland,

—, *Creed and Character.* London 1887. Read Books 2008. General Books 2010.

—, *Logic and Life.* London 1882. Ulan Press 2012. HardPress 2013.

F.J.A. Hort, *The Christian Ecclesia.* London: Macmillan 1897. HardPress 2013, etc.

H.E. Hopkins, *Morning and Evening Prayer.* London: Hodder & Stoughton 1963.

Ted Hughes, *Shakespeare and the Goddess of Complete Being.* London: Faber 1993 / 2021.

J.R. Illingworth,

—, *Personality, Human and Divine.* London: Macmillan 1894. HardPress 2013, etc.

—, *Divine Imminence.* London: Macmillan 1898. Read Books 2007.

—, *Divine Transcendence.* London: Macmillan 1911. Kessinger 2003.

C.G. Jung, 'The Development of Personality' in *Collected Works*, Vol. 17. London: Routledge/ Princeton Univ. Press 1991.

William Kay, *The Psalms: Translated from the Hebrew with notes chiefly exegetical.* London, Oxford & Cambridge: Rivingtons 1874².

Carl Kemper, *Der Bau.* Stuttgart: Verlag Freies Geistesleben 2007.

G.A. Studdert Kennedy, *The New Man in Christ.* London 1932. Read Books 2007.

Hertha Kluge-Kahn, *Johann Sebastian Bach; die verschlüsselten theologischen Aussagen in seinem Spätwerk* (Wolfenbüttel and Zürich: Möseler 1985). E.T. in MS by A.S. 'Bach, God and Number'. On the solo violin works, see www.helga-thoene.de

Milo Mahan,

—, 'Mystic Numbers' in *The Collected Works*, Vol. 2. New York: Pott, Young & Co. 1875.

—, *Palmoni, or the Numerals of Scripture, a Proof of Inspiration.* BiblioLife 2009. Forgotten Books 2012. http://archive.org/details/palmoniorthenume00mahauoft

George Matheson,

—, 'Originality of the Character of Christ'. *The Contemporary Review*, Vol. XXXIII. Aug.-Nov. 1878. London: Strahan, pp. 758-775.

—, 'The Promise of Revelation', *The Monthly Interpreter* 1886: 146-154.

—, *Studies of the Portrait of Christ*, 2 vols. London: Hodder & Stoughton 1900/1901. BiblioLife 2009; Rarebookclub 2012, Forgotten Books 2018, etc. (Through inner observation, creative paraphrase, 'the blind seer of Scotland' poetically portrays the mind of Christ in non-specialist language; a new benchmark in devotional literature.)

—, *Moments on the Mount*. London, Nisbet 1884. BiblioBazaar 2009. Ulan Press 2012. Hardpress 2013.

John Michell, *City of Revelation*. Garnstone Press, London 1972/78.

John Michell and Christine Rhone, *Twelve-Tribe Nations*. Inner Traditions 2008.

Hans Nissen. Der Sinn des 'Wohltemperierten Klaviers II. Teil'. *Bach-Jahrbuch* 1951/52. 54-80. Online: https://doi.org/10.13141/bjb.v19521567 (some typos are apparent, e.g. numbers of bars.)

Stephen Prickett, *Words and the Word*. Cambridge: CUP 1986.

O.C. Quick, *The Christian Sacraments*. London: Nisbet 1927/ Collins, Fontana 1964.

Arthur Michael, Ramsey, *From Gore to Temple; The Development of Anglican Theology 1889-1939*. Wipf and Stock, 2009.

Christoph Rau,

—, *The Four around the One*, tr. A.S. SteinerBooks, forthcoming.

—, *Struktur und Rhythmus im Johannes-Evangelium*. Stuttgart: Urachhaus 1972.

—, *Das Matthäus-Evangelium*. Stuttgart: Urachhaus 1976.

Wilfrid Richmond,

—, *Experience: A Chapter of Prolegomena*. London: Swan Sonnenschein 1896. http://archive.org/details/experienceachap00richgoog (brief & lucid; the missing ending in the online version is to be found in 'Reviews', initial page, below right).

—, *An Essay on Personality,* London: Arnold 1900/ Kessinger 2010/ Ulan Press 2012 (worthy to stand beside *The Philosophy of Freedom*)

John A.T. Robinson,

—, *The Body*. London: SCM 1952.

—, *Thou Who Art,* Intro. Abp. Rowan Williams. Continuum 2006 (Robinson's brilliant Ph.D. thesis, extracted from the vaults of Cambridge Univ. Lib., prepared & ed. by A.S., foreign words tr. by Margaret Barker—both volunteer editors & the final editor who also prepared the Index etc. unacknowledged by the publisher).

Adolph Saphir, *Our Lord's Pattern of Prayer.* Nisbet 1872 / Grand Rapids: Kregel 1984.

W. Robertson Smith, *The Old Testament in the Jewish Church.* London: A&C Black 1892. Ulan Press 2012. HardPress 2013.

Rudolf Steiner:—most of the Collected Works (GA–*Gesamtausgabe*) are available online: http://www.rsarchive.org (Germ. http://fvn-archiv.net/PDF/GA)

—, 'Faith, Love, Hope', lecture Nuremberg, 2 Dec. 1911, in *The Golden Blade,* London 1964: 1-26 https://waldorflibrary.org/journals/164-golden-blade/

—, *Goethe as Founder of a New Science of Aesthetics* (Botton, ND), also included in R. Steiner, *Art as Spiritual Activity,* ed. M. Howard. Anthroposophic Press, Spring Valley 1998.

—, *Eurythmy as Visible Speech* (GA 279). Tr. & commentary by A.S. RSP 2019.

—, *Eurythmy as Visible Singing* (GA 278). Tr. & commentary by A.S. RSP 2019[5].

—, Vorträge und Kurse über christlich-religiöses Wirken IV, Vom Wesen des wirkenden Wortes, GA 345, Dornach 1994.

William Temple,

—, *Mens Creatrix.* London: Macmillan 1917. Kessinger 2010. HardPress 2013.

—, *Nature, Man and God.* London 1934. Kessinger 2010 (see also A.S. on Dr Temple, in *Perspectives* Oct./Nov. 1994. 6-9 Dec. 1994/Jan. 1995. 4-6).

Helga Thoene. To date, Frau Thoene has published detailed analytical studies on the G-minor Sonata (Cöthener Bach-Hefte 6, Veröffentlichungen des Historischen Museums Köthen/Anhalt 19. Köthen, 1994), D-minor Chaconne (dr. ziethen verlag, Oschersleben 2003), the A-minor (2005) & C-major Sonatas (2008) helga-thoene.de/C.C. Torrey,

—, *The Four Gospels*. London/ New York 1933 (http://archive.org/details/fourgospels00torruoft)

—, *Our Translated Gospels: Some of the Evidence*. London/ New York. 1936.

—, *The Apocalypse of John*. Newhaven: Yale 1958.

Allan Becher Webb, *Unveiling the Eternal Word*. London 1897 (retreat addresses: http://anglicanhistory.org/africa/za/abwebb/unveiling1897.html uploaded by A.S.)

John Wesley, *Explanatory Notes upon the New Testament*. London: Epworth Press 1950; reprinted Forgotten Books 2012.

Michael Ward,

—, *Planet Narnia: The Seven Heavens in the Imagination of C.S. Lewis*. Oxford: OUP 2008.

—, *The Narnia Code: C.S. Lewis and the Secret of the Seven Heavens*. Milton Keynes: Paternoster 2010 (a more popular account).

Dom H. van Zeller, *Approach to Prayer*. London and New York: Sheed & Ward 1958; possibly reissued as *Prayer and the Will of God*. Sophia Institute Press 2003.

Further Reading

1) Hermann Beckh, *Collected Articles 1922-1938* (Temple Lodge 2023), e.g.:

   No. 7, 'The Act of Consecration of Man and the Meaning of Life', 77-81.

   No. 21, 'Meeting with Rudolf Steiner', 180-88, esp. p. 187f.

   No. 41, 'Michaelmas in The Act of Consecration of Man', 344-50.

2) Rudolf Frieling, *Experiencing Renewal (1925-1982): Studies in Liturgy, Number and John's Gospel* (Temple Lodge 2024), includes Frieling's contributions on the Epistles, also a study on the ACM by Fr. Rittelmeyer and another by H. Beckh:

Contents

Foreword

Early Contributions

   The Destruction of the Temple and the End of the World (1925)

   Christ in John's Gospel (1926)

   Friedrich Rittelmeyer: Right Worship (1926)

Sacred Playing (1925)

   1. Sacred Playing

   2. The Three Steps

   3. The Liturgical Colours

   4. Sacred Numbers

   5. Time and Space

Prayer and the Renewed Sacrament (1929-1975)

   Foreword by Sigrid Lindström (2002)

   1. The Earth—Exile or Homeland?

   2. Beginning

   3. The Beginning of the Christian Church

   4. Metamorphoses of the Christian Eurcharist

   5. The Seven Sacraments in the developing Consciousness of Christianity's History

   6. The Step in Consciousness to meet the Liturgical Ritual

3) Günter Dellbrügger, *Im Herzland: Zur Esoterik des christlichen Jahres*. Urachhaus 2016. Eng. tr. Floris Books, Edinburgh, forthcoming (2025). On the liturgical Epistles of the ACM with facsimiles, texts and Rudolf Frieling's contributions.

4) See also, Alan Stott, 'The Rhythm of Freedom: Rudolf Steiner's "dry, mathmatical style"', in *Hermann Beckh: A Celebration*, TL (2025).

About the Author

ALAN STOTT (b. 1949) first experienced the yearly cycle of The Act of Consecration of Man, London 1967-68, with the team ministry under Dr Alfred Heidenreich—with Dr Ferdinand Rauter (piano), co-founder of the Anglo-Austrian Music Society (1942). From lessons with Dr Rauter, he learnt that an accompanist must be 'twice the musician'. As a server, Alan soon learnt the renewed liturgy. Impulses received from musicians' meetings in London chaired by Dr Heidenreich are decisive for a lifetime. From Dr Heidenreich, Ormand Edward and Eileen Hersey he gained a respect for British theology; from Irene Taylor social awareness and guidance in the meditative life; under George Klockner's direction he took part in Shakespeare plays; from a conference with Adam Bittleston he heard about the noble Eightfold Path. Decades later, Alan translated for *Perspectives* (Mar./May 2002–Sept./Nov. 2003) Christoph Rau's articles on Luke's Gospel and the Eightfold Path; this led to the discovery of this down-to-earth Path—aiming to achieve a balance between Heaven and Earth—is hidden in the admonitions and jokes of Steiner's eight eurythmy lectures (GA 278; see study-edition RSP 2019, Appendix 9).

Alan co-founded the Bristol Waldorf School 1974, serving for some years at The Christian Community early on Tuesdays and playing on Sunday mornings. In 1977 Alan cycled to the Priests Seminary, Stuttgart. In Germany, however, he led an active musical life for seven years, playing intensively for eurythmy. In addition to the countless students and children from whom he learnt, including many piano students, an artistic high-point was the three years with Friedhelm & Ursula-Ingrid Gillert in the Eurythmy Training, Munich, and touring throughout Europe with the Eurythmy Stage Group, Munich.

Formally, Alan probably learnt most as a player in a single four-hour lesson with the pianist Robert Kolben (Munich). Compositions, Kolben taught, portray 'spiritual situations'; this musician knew Beethoven in particular from within.

Alan met Maren at the Eurythmy School Nuremberg (1980), and they formed an artistic duo in England (1982). They felt a common task beckoning, and in 1983 Maren took his surname and became Alan's better half ever since, playing for services (flute and piano), teaching, performing eurythmy—eventually in five continents. They founded 'Anderida Ensemble', performed in several annual Community Meetings and regularly at Christian Community centres, including London West and, for several Christmas Conferences, Forest Row, Sussex—until the policy there regarding eurythmy performances changed. Together they have attended numerous annual Christian Community Conferences for Priests and Musicians, meeting significant personalities; together, too, they have translated from the German several works by priests of The Christian Community (Fr. Rittelmeyer, H. Beckh, R. Frieling, Chr. Rau, R. Meyer, K. Von Wistinghausen, many still in MS), some important studies on music (Hermann Beckh, Hertha Kluge-Kahn, Hermann Pfrogner, and Christoph Peter), language and eurythmy, numerous issues of the *Newsletter: Section for the Performing Arts* (Dornach 1996–2016) and four titles in Rudolf Steiner's Collected Works (GA 277a, 278, 279, and 315). The study-edition of Steiner's *Eurythmy as Visible Singing*, is now in its fifth edition (Temple Lodge 2019); its companion volume is *Eurythmy as Visible Speech* (TL 2019). Composers Nigel Osborne and Howard Skempton have written works for this performing duo (2012).

Since 1991, Alan performs with Eurythmy West Midlands, works as a musician, playing, leading the choir and tutoring at the Eurythmy School, Glasshouse Arts Centre, Stourbridge-UK, www.eurythmywm.org.uk, and as a translator, editor and writer. He edited John Docherty's seminal study *The Literary Products of the Lewis Carroll–George MacDonald Friendship* (Edwin Mellen Press 1995, 1997²). From a Cambridge library vault he salvaged John A.T. Robinson's remarkable thesis *Thou Who Art*, edited the text and prepared the disc for publication (Introduction by Archbishop Rowan Williams, Continuum 2006).

That Steiner was the first to solve the Mystery of who wrote Shakespeare was first argued in 'Shakespeare—Who held the Pen? Insights meets research', *Shakespeare Matters*, Summer 2007, and a sequel

'Shakespeares—Treason or Transformation? *Shakespeare Matters;* Fall 2011, online: https://www.shakespeareoxfordfellowship.org/shakespeare-matters-newsletter/ 'Something cannot be. Only it is: Beyond the Murder of Gonzago' in *Section Newsletter: Section for the Performing Arts* (RB 47, Dornach, Michaelmas 2007); a shorter version in German, 'Wer war Shakespeare?' in *Das Goetheanum* (28 January 2012, Nr. 4: 4-7).

Earlier, with Julian Pook, Alan organized Music Conferences, collected, edited and supplemented music written in the British Isles for the renewed Sacraments during the first 100 years; some of Alan's congregational songs and children's songs edited by Julian Pook are sung in English-speaking centres around the globe (both *Congregational Songs* and *Piano Cycle* pub. by Upper Esk Music (distributor: alanstotty@gmail.com). This musician organized local confirmees, friends and musicians into duos, trios and quartets for special occasions. Upon request, he led the music for the countrywide celebration of the first 70 years of The Christian Community in Britain with a cantata, 'A Wedding', libretto loosely based on Matt. 22; it involved everyone who was present, including Taco Bay and Hans-Werner Schroeder from Stuttgart (Forest Row 1999). His session had to follow—what everyone was fearing, and in fact turned out to be—the last and moving talk by Rev. Rachel Shepherd. She paid homage to John Henry, Cardinal Newman (1801-1890), the leading 19th century writer of English prose—born long before his time, according to Steiner (London, 24 April 1922, GA 211)—who championed the laity,[32] and Cardinal Hume (1923-1999), a gentle Benedictine man of prayer who had recently crossed the threshold and whom, she suggested, had been an—or even *the*—unacknowledged spiritual leader of the country.

Since the turn of the millennium, despite the national and international steady exodus of musicians who shake their heads, Maren and Alan managed some more years volunteering their best to contribute church music in The Christian Community in Great Britain. They have also translated many titles on music and theology. Study of the New Testament and its inspiration has always beckoned. It provides its own context, in particular what the Apostle to the Gentiles[33] (Fig. on next page: Mosaic of Paul, Ravenna) wrote in the first century, in a twenty-first-century version. Take, for example, the following passage:

St Paul

Does it sound like we're patting ourselves on the back, insisting on our credentials, asserting our authority? Well, we're not. Neither do we need letters of endorsement, either to you or from you, You yourselves are all the endorsement we need. Your very lives are a letter ['epistle': AV/KJV] that anyone can read by just looking at you. Christ himself wrote it—not with ink, but with God's living Spirit; not chiselled into stone but carved into human lives—and we publish it.

Soli Del Gloria (motto of Bach, Handel and others)